Rethinking
"Getting Serious about Getting Married"

Rethinking
"Getting Serious about Getting Married"

A Biblical Response to Debbie Maken's Book and to the Assault on Unmarried Men by Religious Leaders

Copyright © 2008 by the Author. Some rights reserved.

All scripture quotations, unless otherwise indicated, are taken from the New King James Version®. Copyright © 1982 by Thomas Nelson, Inc. Used by permission. All rights reserved.

Scripture quotations marked (ESV) are from The Holy Bible, English Standard Version®, copyright © 2001 by Crossway Bibles, a publishing ministry of Good News Publishers. Used by permission. All rights reserved.

The author gives permission for this book to be freely reproduced in its entirety without alteration provided this notice of permission is retained. Quotations from other sources are either used by permission or are provided under the doctrine of fair use for the purposes of criticism and/or scholarship, and remain the intellectual property of their respective authors with all rights reserved.

ISBN: 978-0-557-01787-4

TABLE OF CONTENTS

PREFACE
ix

PART I
(Debbie Maken's Introduction to Her Book)
1

PART II
(Ch. 1 - "What the Bible Says About Marriage")
3

PART III
(Ch. 2 - "What the Bible Says About Being Single")
9

PART IV
(Ch. 3 - "Historical Views on Singleness")
17

PART V
(Ch. 4 - "The Lack of Male Leadership: The True Cause of Protracted Singleness")
21

PART VI
(Ch. 5 - "What We've Been Taught")
35

PART VII
(Ch. 6 - "The 'Gift' of Singleness and the Sovereignty of God")
37

PART VIII
(Ch. 7 - "'Wait on the Lord'")
41

PART IX
(Ch. 8 - "'Jesus Is All You Need'")
47

PART X
(Ch. 9 - "'Being Single = Knowing and Serving God Better'")
53

PART XI
(Ch. 10 - "'Single = Celibate'")
57

PART XII
(Ch. 11 - "A Few More 'Easy' Answers")
71

PART XIII
(Ch. 12 - "Saying No to the Dating Game")
75

Table of Contents

PART XIV
(Ch. 13 - "Enlisting Agency")
83

PART XV
(Ch. 14 - "Inspiring Men to Biblical Manhood")
97

PART XVI
(Conclusion)
105

NOTES
115

PREFACE

What you have before you is a critical review of Debbie Maken's book, *Getting Serious about Getting Married*. Why this review and why the big deal? Simple. Many changes that have taken place over the last several decades have impacted the way men relate to women and have impacted any prospects men have of being happily married. As a man, I am concerned about the fallout of these changes and what they mean for men of today and men of tomorrow. It is true that Mrs. Maken's book is primarily directed towards a female audience, but unfortunately most of her ire is aimed at men. I believe that she has become the poster girl for those voices in our churches who want to tar and feather men for the difficulty women now face in getting married. The circulation and popularity of her book merely reinforces my suspicion that the gynocentrism and misandry of the larger culture has found its way even among Evangelicals. I fear that if enough people buy into Mrs. Maken's message, the religious prejudice now directed at single men will only intensify. That is why I refuse to be silent.

It is true that my book, in its final form, comes over two years after the publication of Mrs. Maken's book. Perhaps some of the initial furor that surrounded her book has indeed died down. However, a man does not need to even read her book to appreciate the issues I raise in my review. Though the proverbial fifteen minutes of fame given to Mrs. Maken's book may come to an end, the attitudes and sentiments expressed by her about men have been and continue to be expressed by others.

There is a movement afoot among some religious leaders to pressure single people, but especially men, to marry. The "Marriage Mandate Movement," as it is now referred to by some, has gone so far as to even declare that singleness on the part of men is sinful in some cases. There are other teachings surrounding this movement that also cause me alarm. One is the notion that married people sin if they do not want to have children. Another idea is that men are the ones who must take the initiative in any amorous relationship they might have with women. These teachings and similar beliefs are, in my estimation, unscriptural, ridiculous, and insulting to men.

At the very least, I deny any necessity placed on the act of marriage for most people. The statement that "God expects most people to marry" is a statement of presumption and conjecture. There is nothing in the Scriptures to indicate that God has marriage in mind for most people today. The matter falls under God's permissive will (what he allows people to do). Since marriage and singleness, per se, are equally valid choices as far the Scriptures are concerned, God can work to his glory through man's exercise of free will in this regard. Marriage may be a blessing, but individuals need not pursue it any more than they need to pursue eating meats (Rom. 14:1-23). Maybe most people will choose to marry, but an increasing number of people are not doing so. Specifically, in a crass, anti-male, anti-family, dehumanizing, materialistic society, we should not be surprised when a large number of men decide that marriage offers them little if anything positive. I discuss this matter at length as well other related issues in my book. This is why I believe men should read what I have to say whether they are familiar with Debbie Maken or not.

Further Remarks about My Book

This book has its genesis in some posts I made at my old blog Scripturally Single (scipturallysingle.blogspot.com) under the pen name of "Anakin Niceguy" between June 2006 and April 2007. The core of my book consists of sixteen "parts," which basically correspond to the chapters in Debbie Maken's work. I have made several edits to my material, primarily with regard to grammar and style. Among the changes I have made is the reformatting of all citations to appear as endnotes. The exceptions to this rule are Bible verses and citations to Debbie Maken's book, which appear as parenthetical references. The endnotes are listed in the "Notes" section at the back of my book.

Some acknowledgments are in order. First, I want to thank my readers at the Scripturally Single blog for their feedback on my original posts. Fans and critics alike have, as far I am concerned, made this book what it is. I want to thank the men of the MGTOW movement for shining a light on some uncomfortable truths about gender issues when so many others in our government, schools, workplaces, media, and churches are not willing to do so. I want to express my indebtedness to my professors in graduate school who imparted unto me the necessary skills for biblical exegesis. The education I received in that regard has helped me defend the truth in this book. Most importantly, I want to thank God for permitting me to put my thoughts down in writing. I pray that what I have said is according to his will and that it will further his interests.

September 2008

PART I

Debbie Maken's Introduction to Her Book
(Disaster Ground Zero)

Getting Serious about Getting Married. This is the book by Debbie Maken that is supposed to cause a sea change in Evangelical thought about singleness and marriage. No longer are we to excuse singleness as an acceptable lifestyle for most people. On contrary, most Christians (and especially men) are supposed to heed God's call to "be fruitful and multiply."

On the back cover of Debbie Maken's book, there is a quote from Albert Mohler, president of Southern Baptist Theological Seminary: "Now comes Debbie Maken with sound advice, serious thinking, and an honest approach to this question that will help all Christians think about our responsibility to get serious about getting married. This book should be a must-read for all Christian young adults—and for all who love them." So is this book a "must read" for "all" Christian young adults? I decided to give it a read. It soon became apparent, however, that this book is not for all Christian young adults. In fact, the book was not meant to be *for* me, but to be *about* me ... as a man. It holds those of my demographic out as the punching bags for Mrs. Maken's intended readers. Her target audience is *single women*, and the book is little more than a pep rally for the same. Mrs. Maken's publisher may refer to her as an "Esther" (p. 9) but at best, I find her to be an Esther without a cause.

In the introduction of her book, Mrs. Maken tells about how her life was in her early twenties. She declares, among other things, that she didn't initially mind being single. After all, she was attractive, intelligent, and likeable (p. 11). What are we to make of this? Here we have a young woman that is materially blessed in so many ways that very few people of either sex are. She goes on to talk about her "rotating boyfriends" who were "mostly frogs who refused to become princes" (Ibid.), so we cannot assume that she was failing to receive any attention from men. It is at this point, at the very outset of the book, that I've lost sympathy for Mrs. Maken. Her statements are very akin to what the Apostle John would describe as the "boasting" of what one "has and does" (1 John 2:16). I could frankly care less about her worldly achievements, so why does she belabor them ("I was cute enough, smart enough, ...")? Here, her narrative smacks of self-importance and detracts from the main points of her book.

She spends the rest of the Introduction bewailing her singleness that she experienced well into her late twenties (although many have been single for a lot longer than that). On page 15, she tell us that God showed her that she "was never going to get true spiritual peace about singleness" because she wasn't "called to singleness", and that "the Spirit does not give peace about something that is outside of God's calling." Perhaps the Spirit does not give peace in something outside of God's calling, but I find myself curious about Mrs. Maken's statement just the same. How did Mrs. Maken arrive at her conclusion? Was it through a hunch or some form of intuition? Did she hunt for Bible proof-texts later on to justify a stance she already purposed in her heart to take? The reason I ask these questions is because the Bible warns against the heart being a guide in religion (Jer. 17:9).

Elsewhere in the Introduction, Mrs. Maken alludes to some social research that supposedly proves married people are happier, healthier, and wealthier than single people. But this ignores other research that suggests only one in four marriages are happy,[1] and that unhappy marriages are detrimental to self-esteem and health.[2] There is also at least one study that suggests that happily married people are not happier because they married, per se, but because happy people are already prone to matrimony.[3] If only marriage was the panacea that some make it out to be.

At any rate, Mrs. Maken adjures us: "As you read, let Scripture be your measuring stick for truth—not psychology, not culture, not what you accepted thus far, not what sounds good or catchy" (p. 16). How ironic that I find that the exact opposite is true with Mrs. Maken's book: it relies on psychology, acceptance of cultural norms, and yes—what sounds good and catchy (especially in her characterization of single men). As for where I think Mrs. Maken's book stands in regard to a sound exegesis of the Bible, I will address that concern in the following sections of my critique.

PART II

Chapter 1
"What the Bible Says About Marriage"
(God's Blessing or Mrs. Maken's Commandment?)

In the first chapter of *Getting Serious about Getting Married*, Debbie Maken lays forth her case that marriage is prescribed by the Bible for most people. She states that "God does not change" and what people "learn about him from the Bible—whether in Genesis, Joel, James—is just as relevant for us today as it was in the past" (p. 22). But such an observation misses the point. I agree that God's nature does not change, but his expectations for humanity most certainly *have*.

Many people, believers and unbelievers alike, are ignorant of the fact that the Bible is a book of four religions, each expressing a covenant God made with an elect group of people. We have the religion of Adam and Eve, the religion of the Patriarchs (Noah, Abraham, etc.), the religion of the Jews, and finally the religion of the Christians. A crucial event paved the way from one spiritual epoch to another: the Fall, Mount Sinai, and the Cross. There can be no going back to a previous set of expectations. Contrary to what Mrs. Maken might claim, there is no way back to Eden. If anyone questions what I have said, they need to read the book of Hebrews, for example, and see what God has to say about those who try to follow the Old Testament. Bear this in mind as you consider my review of Mrs. Maken's claims.

Marriage and Loneliness

One of Mrs. Maken's proof texts is Genesis 2:18. Here we read that "it is not good for the man to be alone." Which man is the Scriptures describing here? Adam. A "helpmeet" was made for *him*. Many commentators, including Mrs. Maken, want to point to Genesis 2:18 as being a normative statement on marriage in general. That is, at best, debatable. Look at the text again. God did not say "it is not good for man to be unmarried." He said it is not good for "*the* man" to be "*alone*." Adam was indeed alone in the sense that no other human being on earth ever was or will be.

Even if we understand Adam's state of being "alone" as referring to his marital status, God's comments are with respect to *Adam in particular*, not necessarily to *men in general*. For if we declare that *men in general* are under purview in this passage, then there can be no exceptions for singleness. Why? Because the Bible never encourages people to embrace that which God declares to be "not good." However, since Mrs. Maken concedes that some people *are encouraged* by the Bible to be single under some circumstances, then she must either call "good" what God says is "not good" or concede that Genesis 2:18 has a limited application. What limited application shall we embrace? Let the Bible speak for itself: "I will make *him* a help meet for *him* [Adam]" (ASV).

Mrs. Maken goes on to write: "Had God intended a buddy system of friends and family to be a happy compromise in the fight against aloneness, he could have simply made more people from the available dust and removed Adam's loneliness through community" (p. 24). This statement is about as compelling as saying, "Had God intended for most everyone to be happily married, we could just fall asleep and wake up to a spouse and a missing rib." Neither assertion is substantive, because conjecture about the mind of God and the alternatives he might have otherwise picked is no substitute for exegeting the Scriptures.

There is one other matter to consider: God's plans for marriage in heaven —that is, *no marriage* (Matt. 22:30). In both the beginning and at the end of history, we find God in perfect fellowship with humanity. We cannot assume that marriage was created for a fallen world because we find it instituted in an ideal world (Eden). However, we also cannot assume it is essential to an ideal world, per se, because it will not be part of the Resurrection. If marriage, per se, is not a provision for a sinful world nor an essential component of an ideal word, then what is it for? As it is, we cannot say with any certainty that the purpose marriage fulfilled in the Garden of Eden is one that it needs to fulfill today or one it fulfills in the life to come.

Marriage and Work

Mrs. Maken claims that marriage was designed to give meaning to work. This is a peculiar notion because God did not say, "I will make a suitable rationale for Adam to work." On the contrary, Eve is referred as a "helpmeet" to assist Adam in the work that was *already* purposed for him. Mrs. Maken confuses the means with the end. Woman is not the focus of man's work; God is. We work in order to glorify Him (1 Cor. 10:31). If work is so dependent on marriage for meaning, shall we exempt singles from their labors until they get married? Why not? As it is, there are scriptural reasons to work in spite of marriage (2 Thess. 3:10; Eph. 4:28; Eccl. 2:24).

Marriage and Children

It is beyond the scope of this review to address the issue of whether or not God commands married people to have children. Suffice it to say, if God does not command marriage of everyone, it is a logical conclusion that the same can be said about children. And that brings us to a favorite proof-text of Mrs. Maken and many other religionists: Genesis 1:28. In this passage, we read where God said, "Be fruitful and multiply." Unfortunately, it seems that too many commentators ignore a few words that precede that statement (viz., "And God said unto *them*"). Why should we suppose that a wish for two people to be "fruitful and multiply" applies with equal force to six billion? It is also worthy to note that in Genesis 9:1 and 9:7, God does not say, "Let every man be fruitful and multiply." The addressees in these verses are also specified: four men alone on a planet with their wives.

Mrs. Maken's Reading of Malachi 2:15

Apart from Genesis 1:28, Mrs. Maken takes comfort in Malachi 2:15. On page 27, she quotes the ESV: "Did he not make them one, with a portion of the Spirit in their union? And what was the one God seeking? Godly offspring. So guard yourselves in your spirit, and let none of you be faithless to the wife of your youth." One may come away form this verse believing God wants people to marry and have children in order to bring more believers into the world.

There's just one problem. Malachi 2:15 is a notoriously difficult passage to translate from the original language. John Calvin, one of Mrs. Maken's favorite religious figures, conceded as much (though his interpretation seems to support Mrs. Maken's reading of the passage).[1] When conservative scholars admit there are serious textual problems with the Hebrew manuscripts of Malachi 2:15, we should not be surprised when our English Bibles manifest a variance in translation. Let us look at some of the English versions of the Bible that *do not* support Mrs. Maken's reading of Malachi 2:15 ...

1. The following translations mention God "seeking godly offspring" but do not make any reference to marriage in the Garden of Eden. Therefore, Malachi 2:15 could be just referring to the children of *Jews* in particular as opposed to humanity in general:

- New Revised Standard Version
- Revised English Bible
- New English Bible
- Douay-Rheims
- New Living Translation
- New American Bible
- Holman Christian Standard Bible

2. The following translations don't even specify God "seeking godly offspring" much less mention anything about marriage in the Garden of Eden:

- The Peshitta (Lamsa translation of Ancient Near Eastern Manuscripts of the Bible)
- New American Standard Bible
- American Standard Version (the alternate reading)
- English Standard Version (the alternate reading—from the version that Mrs. Maken quotes)

We see that those of Mrs. Maken's persuasion can ill-afford to be dogmatic about their position. However, if one wants to latch on to some possible gloss of the text, then it is best to look at the context and take the most plausible reading. Which reading shall we embrace? I agree with one scholar's understanding of Malachi 2:15: "The phrase *zera' 'elohim* ['godly seed'] connects in the most meaningful way to the preceding verse if it is used as a designation for the offspring resulting from the marriages of the *addressed men*. According to the prophet, this offspring constitutes 'godly seed' *only if the children are born out of the relation between members of the YHWH-congregation and Israelite wives*, whereas the children born by women of foreign faiths cannot be called 'godly seed.'"[2]

Unlike the Israelites, Christians do not constitute a physical kingdom, but a spiritual one. In a spiritual kingdom, "godly seed" does not come by physical means, but by spiritual means (Mark 4:30–32; Matt. 28:18–20; 1 Peter 1:22–23). I understand my remarks on Malachi 2:15 may seem like overkill, but the passage is a popular proof-text for religious pundits who promote marriage and childbearing. That Mrs. Maken or anyone else would try to make a such modern day application of Malachi 2:15 is simply unwarranted.

The Natural Law Flaw

Near the end of chapter 1, Mrs. Maken makes the following statement: "Natural law simply means the 'way something is made is the way it should act'" (p. 27). Thus, Mrs. Maken assumes that it is just "natural" for us to marry and have children. Obviously, the fact that we are created "male and female" points to the design of marriage being the norm early in humanity's history. However, *what else* was the norm for human beings in the Garden of Eden? The norm was that they were "naked and unashamed." Innocence allowed for sexuality's *full expression*. There were no unpleasant repercussions. If we want to look at nature, as Mrs. Maken suggests, then we must look at animals who wear no clothing and have no artificial constraint on their sexuality.

Indeed, the proponents of "natural law" sound, at times, very much like Darwinists. Of course, Evangelical "natural law" proponents would never encourages us to do what "comes natural." Many fall back on their Calvinistic position of total heredity depravity to explain that our natures are flawed by sin. But there is nothing flawed or sinful about being "naked and unashamed," per se, so why do we cover up?

We see from the matter of nakedness that people must, at times, forego even that which was originally declared good in God's eyes. The same holds true for marriage. The issues of nakedness, sex, marriage, and reproduction stand or fall together. If the Fall necessitates constraints on any one of these, then the same holds true for others. We live in a fallen world of scarcity, poverty, hunger, stress, pain, disease, sadness, covetousness, hatred, and death. If nakedness and sex are not unqualified blessings, then neither are marriage and children (Prov. 30:21, 23a; Luke 21:23).

Conclusion about Chapter 1

Mrs. Maken's comments about marriage in the Garden of Eden are proof of nothing except how things might have been under more ideal circumstances. It seems that she wants us to embrace marriage enthusiastically and unreservedly regardless of what the Fall did. If we are going to expect human beings to replicate one component of the Edenic experience in such a manner, then perhaps in addition to promoting marriage, we should join a nudist colony. Needless to say, I won't hold my breath for any to take me up on that offer.

PART III

Chapter 2
"What the Bible Says About Being Single"
(So What Kind of Eunuch Are You, Dude?)

What does the Bible say about single people? In the second chapter of *Getting Serious about Getting Married*, Debbie Maken attempts to answer this question. However, as in chapter 1, I find that her exegesis misses the mark.

Jesus and Matthew 19:11–12

A key text Mrs. Maken cites for her claim that most people must get married is Matthew 19:11–12. Here, we have Jesus discussing a group of people who should not marry. Are we to assume that the people Jesus mentions are an exclusive class who alone have the right to be single? Is everyone else nonexempt from marriage? Debbie Maken apparently thinks so. Speaking of Matthew 19:11–12 and 1 Corinthians 7, she says, "People who don't meet the singleness requirements are under the general rule that God established in Genesis" (p. 29).

However, let's look closely at Matthew 19:11–12. Jesus did not say, "Not everyone can be single except for a select group." He said, "All cannot receive *this saying*, but only those to whom it was given ..." (v. 11). What was the "saying" that not everyone could receive? The "saying" in question was the disciples statement in verse 10: "If such is the case of man with his wife, it is better not to marry." A more literal translation would be: "It is *not good* to marry."

There is an issue here that Mrs. Maken has overlooked (although to be fair to her, other commentators have probably overlooked it as well). If Jesus rejects the statement that "it is *not good* to marry" with only a few exceptions in mind, are we to assume that everyone else is *required* to marry? The answer is No. Let us not commit the logical fallacy of posing a false dilemma. Readers should take note: When Jesus rejected the disciples' notion that marriage is "*not good*," he did *not* reject the notion that singleness *is good*. If either marriage or singleness were bad, then God would not recommend either state for *anyone*. As it is, the Bible affirms that *both* marriage and singleness, in principal, *are good* (1 Cor. 7:38).

The people Jesus addresses in Matthew 19:12 are people for which the saying "it is *not good* to marry" holds true in a way that it does not hold true for others. They are eunuchs either in the literal sense or the figurative sense. Indeed, very few single people fall into the category considered here. For many other people, it is good to be *either single or married*. Granted, there are those of whom it can be said, "It is *not good* to *be single*." I refer, of course, to people who are *already married*, for matrimony definitely comes with obligations (1 Cor. 7:2–7). But conceding this is not akin to embracing the kind of far-reaching claims that Mrs. Maken makes about the need to get married.

So, What Kind of Eunuch Am I, Mrs. Maken?

Having established that Jesus did not place restrictions on singleness, per se, in Matthew 19:11–12, let us therefore consider Mrs. Maken's remarks on page 32. She recalls a date she had with a thirtysomething bachelor and her probative question to him, "So what kind of 'eunuch' are you?" Mrs. Maken labors under the impression that this man should have given an account for his singleness. Supposedly, a man who stays single should either be physically unable to fulfill the obligations of marriage or be preoccupied with a special ministry for the kingdom of God. Mrs. Maken's conduct towards the man in question was regrettable, however. Her confrontational demeanor was needless, as it was clearly based on a misunderstanding of what Matthew 19:11–12 teaches. Granted, the passage mentions three types of "eunuchs":

> For there are eunuchs who were born thus from their mother's womb, and there are eunuchs who were made eunuchs by men, and there are eunuchs who have made themselves eunuchs for the kingdom of heaven's sake ...

The first two categories of "eunuchs" refer, of course, to people who are are biologically ill-suited to have conjugal relations. The third category refers to those who are unmarried because of their service to God. It is this last category that merits our attention.

Mrs. Maken claims those who are "eunuchs .. for the kingdom of heaven's sake" are those who have "received a clear direction from God to be single" (p. 32). However, a careful look at Matthew 19:12 reveals something rather interesting. It says the third category of eunuchs "have *made themselves* eunuchs for the kingdom of heaven's sake." In other words, the singles in question exercised *choice* about their status.

This exercise of *free will* flies squarely of the face of any assertion that people have to be "called to singleness" by God. It also indicates that Christians do not need a supernatural "gift" of diminished sexual desire in order to remain pure (although on page 34, Mrs. Maken assumes *a priori* that single people who take on exceptional ministries must have such an endowment). Finally, one should note that the choice of becoming a figurative eunuch undercuts any assertion that people are to "be fruitful and multiply." For if God indeed still commanded people to have children, then there would clear directives on who could remain single and thereby exempt themselves from the command. Mrs. Maken would like us to believe there are clear directives, but we see that Matthew 19:12 shows otherwise. In essence, it is ironic that the very passage Mrs. Maken uses to support her position actually devastates it.

Singles in the Bible

On pages 34 to 36, Mrs. Maken calls attention to some figures in the Bible that were unmarried. She supposes that these individuals support her assertion that people must have a special calling from God in order to be single. What interests me, however, is her mention of the Apostle Paul and Barnabas. I agree with Mrs. Maken that their missionary work would have made married life a difficult proposition. Yet, notice what Paul claims about Barnabas and himself in 1 Corinthians 9:5: "Do we have no right to take along a believing wife, as do also the other apostles, the brothers of the Lord, and Cephas?" Apparently, Paul thought that he had the same *right* as any other red-blooded male Christian had. He must have not been familiar with the theology of some modern commentators who assume the he was mysteriously endowed with a low sex drive or that the Lord gave him no choice in the matter of marriage.

A "Present Distress" over 1 Corinthians 7

I suppose if there is one passage that causes no small amount of consternation for those who take Debbie Maken's position on marriage, it is 1 Corinthians, chapter 7. In this passage, the Bible's commendation of the single lifestyle cannot be any clearer. How then do those who demand most people get married handle this passage? They may do like Mrs. Maken does —explain it away by assuming it only applies to the first century. She claims that Paul's advise must be understand in the context of a contemporaneous persecution (pp. 37-38). Mrs. Maken's approach to 1 Corinthians 7 is not new to me, as I have run across other writers who take the same position. Needless to say, I am not convinced by the line of reasoning employed by Mrs. Maken and others. It seems that Mr. Mrs. Maken and, by extension, the commentators she follows read too much into the phrase "present distress."

Mrs. Maken may claim that "historians uniformly believe" that Paul was addressing famine and persecution in Corinth, but well-respected Bible scholars *do not* "uniformly believe" this. Other commentators, such as C. K. Barrett[1] and Richard Oster[2], believe the "present distress" points to a more generalized tribulation that Christians endure. If we were to concede a temporal understanding of the phrase "present distress," we are still left with the task of explaining Paul's words in verses 29–31, which end with the statement: "For the form of this world is passing away." Paul's focus here is clearly eschatological. Even Simon Kistemaker, a commentator Mrs. Maken selectively cites in support of her position, states: "Whether we are married, cast into sorrow, given to joy, or acquire possessions, Christians *should not become absorbed by them*. They should see the transient nature of these things and know that after having passed through this earthly vale, believers will enter eternity. In this life, then, they ought to prepare themselves for the life after death."[3] Perhaps Mrs. Maken's fans should examine their own personal feelings in light of this statement. At any rate, if Paul's advice to single people in 1 Corinthians 7 stopped at verse 28, I could perhaps grant something to those of Mrs. Maken's persuasion, but verses 29–31 exhibit a shift in subject matter, as do verses 32–38.

The Married vs. the "Eunuchs"

When we come to 1 Corinthians 7:32, we see Paul commencing a general discussion of the differences between married people and single people. Consider the following language of verse 34:

> There is a difference between a wife and a virgin. The unmarried woman cares about the things of the Lord, that she may be holy both in body and in spirit. But she who is married cares about the things of the world—how she may please her husband.

Are we to believe this verse is only talking about times of exceptional distress? Paul's distinction is between the "unmarried" and "married," not between those who are persecuted and those who are not persecuted. Moreover, Paul says nothing about being anxious for the necessities of life here. Instead, we simply have a statement about "pleasing" one's spouse. The word "pleasing" does not connote times of dire distress, even in the original language of the text. Paul then goes on to say:

> And this I say for your own profit, not that I may put a leash on you, but for what is proper, and that you may serve the Lord without distraction. (v. 35)

Paul's application cannot be more clear: he is not proposing a set of statutes and case law for matrimony. His advice indicates that there is a choice in the matter and that he simply desires that the Corinthians be able to "serve the Lord without distraction." If there is any doubt about whether or not Paul leaves the matter of marriage and singleness up to the Christians he addresses, consider the language of verses 37–38:

> But if any man thinks he is behaving improperly toward his virgin, if she is past the flower of youth, and thus it must be, let him do *what he wishes*. He does not sin; let them marry. Nevertheless he who *stands steadfast in his heart*, having no necessity, but has power over his *own will*, and has so *determined in his own heart* that he will keep his virgin, does well. So then, he who gives her in marriage does well, but he who does not give her in marriage does better. (emphasis mine)

I find it puzzling how Mrs. Maken and others could fail to acknowledge the very clear language of the above passage. Here, Paul indicates that the decision to marry is a matter of one's "own heart" and "own will." There is simply no hint of the matter of matrimony being predetermined by divine fiat. In short, God leaves the choice up to us, and by extension, the notion that we are commanded to "be fruitful and multiply" is again swept away in the wake of this passage.

Distresses That Really Are "Present"

Let the reader assume for the sake of argument that all of 1 Corinthians 7:25–40 pertained to an exceptional circumstance, namely persecution or famine. Was the situation that the Corinthians faced so unique and unparalleled in whole history of Christendom that they merited a special exemption from marriage? How dire did life's circumstances have to be before one could refuse matrimony? Mrs. Maken's suppositions to the contrary, the Bible does not give us any details. The text merely says that Paul wanted the Corinthians "to be without care." We cannot make God to be a respecter of persons (Acts 10:34). At the very least, we have to allow for a present-day application of 1 Corinthians 7:25–40, whether it is wholly couched in terms of a "distress" or not. Today's Christians, like the Corinthians, should be able to forego marriage in order "to be without care." Maybe we are not faced with famine and persecution in today's society, but those who want to start families today face many antagonistic forces in the legal, economic, and social realms.

The Battle of the Commentaries

We have already noted that one commentary Mrs. Maken cites (viz., by Simon Kistemaker) does not agree with her overall position on 1 Corinthians 7:25–40. Another work Mrs. Maken uses also does a disservice to the theology of those who share her beliefs. I refer, in particular, to Gordon Fee's commentary on 1 Corinthians. Contrary to what many believe about 1 Corinthians 7:1–9, Fee does not take this passage as an encouragement for single people to marry. He carefully considers the original Greek language of the text and comes to two striking, but correct, conclusions. The first is that 1 Corinthians 7:1–6 is addressed to Christians who are *already married*; the Apostle's exhortation is for husbands and wives to continue to have intimate relations with each other "in order to avoid fornication." The second conclusion worth noting is that 1 Corinthians 7:9 does not hold forth marriage as a solution for youthful desires, per se. The English translation "cannot contain" is inaccurate. The people under consideration are those who *will not practice self-control* and thereby are *already* caught up in the sin of fornication. Hence, the Apostle Paul indicates that marriage is better than being involved in sin, but he does not necessarily indicate it is better than being single.[4]

Granted, I will admit that I do not entirely agree with Fee's conclusions on 1 Corinthians, chapter 7. For instance, Fee, like Debbie Maken, assumes that the gift of which Paul speaks in verse 7 is some exceptional resistance to sexual desire.[5] I have already noted that such a conclusion is strained in light of Paul's statement in 1 Corinthians 9:5. For all one may know, Paul could be referring to the undivided devotion he had to the Lord as a single man (7:32, 35). Such a "gift" of undivided devotion would certainly fit the context of the preceding statements in verses 5–6. Having said this, I agree with Fee when he states:

> The irony of our present situation is that Paul insisted that his own preference, including his reasons for it, were not to be taken as a noose around anyone's neck. Yet we have allowed that very thing to happen. Roman Catholicism has insisted on celibacy for its clergy even though not all are gifted to be so; *on the other hand, many Protestant groups will not ordain the single because marriage is the norm, and the single are not quite trusted*. The answer again lies in our becoming eschatological people who live in the present with such a clear vision of our certain future that we are *free from such anxiety*, and therefore also *free from placing such strictures on others as well as on ourselves*.[6]

I cannot but wonder if Mrs. Maken actually read this portion of Fee's book. All in all, whether it be Bible passages or commentaries, I again note with irony how the very sources Mrs. Maken uses to support her position actually devastate it.

Debbie Maken's Book - The Rest of Chapter 2

When one moves the beyond the faulty exegesis of Mrs. Maken's book on pages 29–40, there is no much left to consider in chapter 2. What is left is a series of assertions which are patently baseless. For instance, with respect to the so-called "biblical criteria for lifelong singleness," she tells us the "Bible requires voluntarily and permanently renouncing marriage and all that goes with it" (p. 41); this, of course, utterly contradicts the very "right" that Apostle Paul claimed for himself in 1 Corinthians 9:5.

Finally, Mrs. Maken closes the chapter with some comments about single men that I find, as a man, to be quite condescending. Such are unfortunately a foretaste of what we will encounter later in the book. Suffice it to say, by the end of chapter 2, Debbie Maken's book is still-born. Devoid of any meaningful and sound exegesis of the Bible, the rest of Mrs. Maken's volume is little more than a conglomeration of historical trivia, colorful suppositions, and diatribe. I shall, nonetheless, attempt to address the rest of Mrs. Maken's book in the following installments of my critique.

PART IV

Chapter 3
"Historical Views on Singleness"
(The Traditions of the Elders)

In continuing my review of Debbie Maken's book, *Getting Serious about Getting Married*, I would like to share with my readers a passage from the New Testament where the Pharisees confront Jesus:

> Then the Pharisees and some of the scribes came together to Him, having come from Jerusalem. Now when they saw some of His disciples eat bread with defiled, that is, with unwashed hands, they found fault. For the Pharisees and all the Jews do not eat unless they wash their hands in a special way, holding the tradition of the elders. When they come from the marketplace, they do not eat unless they wash. And there are many other things which they have received and hold, like the washing of cups, pitchers, copper vessels, and couches. Then the Pharisees and scribes asked Him, "Why do Your disciples not walk according to the tradition of the elders, but eat bread with unwashed hands?" He answered and said to them, "Well did Isaiah prophesy of you hypocrites, as it is written: 'This people honors Me with their lips, but their heart is far from Me. And in vain they worship Me, teaching as doctrines the commandments of men.' For laying aside the commandment of God, you hold the tradition of men—the washing of pitchers and cups, and many other such things you do." (Mark 7:1–8)

Here we have our Lord and Savior clearly condemning the practice of elevating religious traditionalism to the level of God's divine revelation. Religious traditions are *not* a safe and reliable guide in spiritual matters. That is why I find chapter 3 of Debbie Maken's book so disappointing. She spends the entire chapter detailing how notable theologians and religious communities of the past felt about single people. Apparently, the proverbial "cloud of witnesses" of the past stressed the necessity of marriage for most people, and that is supposed to make us think twice about embracing singleness as a lifestyle.

This will probably come as shock to some of my readers, but I will nonetheless ask this simple question: Who cares? The Bible declares, "If anyone speaks, let him speak as the oracles of God" (1 Peter 4:11). Bereft of sound, biblical exegesis, Debbie Maken's cloud of witnesses becomes a puff of presumptuousness. Revered religious figures and Bible-believers of past ages *can be woefully mistaken.*

Quoting the Big Names

I do not think Mrs. Maken would like us to scrutinize the sentiments of the past too closely. She invokes C.S. Lewis' concept of "chronological snobbery," a term used to "describe our feelings of superiority when we glance back at the past" (p. 48). Her reference to such a renown writer is hilarious, given the fact that C. S. Lewis was pretty much a confirmed bachelor until his fifties. Surely all of Lewis' writing, lecturing and teaching would have not precluded him from seeking the companionship of a female. I suspect that if C.S. Lewis were alive today, Mrs. Maken's supporters would probably dismiss him as an immature "cad" unable to live up to their idea of "biblical manhood."

Then there is the matter of John Calvin and Martin Luther. Mr. Mrs. Maken quotes from these two figures extensively on singleness and marriage. Are these men infallible guides in all things pertaining to life and godliness? I wonder if Mrs. Maken would agree with Calvin that heretics should be put to death? Is she familiar with Sebastian Castellio's response to Calvin's views?[1] Indeed, shall we consult the Reformers when writing a treatise on the "Historical Views of Religious Toleration"? Is our modern embrace of religious liberty sinful? Or is the early Reformers' insistence on persecuting those who disagreed with their theology sinful? Take your pick.

Shall we quote Luther on how to treat the Jews?[2] Or perhaps we should consider this adage of Luther on living soberly and righteously:

> Whenever the devil harasses you thus, seek the company of men or drink more, or joke and talk nonsense, or do some other merry thing. Sometimes we must drink more, sport, recreate ourselves, aye, and even sin a little to spite the devil, so that we leave him no place for troubling our consciences with trifles. We are conquered if we try too conscientiously not to sin at all. So when the devil says to you: "Do not drink," answer him: "I will drink, and right freely, just because you tell me not to."[3]

Needless to say, I am certain one can find plenty of loyalists ready to defend the more uncomfortable pronouncements of the Reformers with complex explanations and apologies. That is another issue for another day. My point is that we cannot base faith our faith on dead, uninspired men, no matter how much our religious communities may esteem them.

This Is Not Your Grandmother's Faith

Let us lay aside the foibles of the revered Reformers and consider the sentiments of Bible-believers of the past. Shall we consult them on slavery? How about racial relations? We could sanctimoniously declare that miscegenation were largely frowned upon by Christians of yesteryear, and it was not until very recently that the idea of interracial marriages was tolerated. We could bolster our prejudice against interracial marriages by misquoting scriptures from the Old Testament, just as Mrs. Maken and her followers have done in mandating marriage for most people. What an ironic twist this would be, given that Boundless.org (an Internet site espousing views akin to Mrs. Maken's) recently published a positive piece on interracial relationships.[4]

What about birth control? Mrs. Maken declares on page 57: "For centuries Protestants and Catholics shared the belief that birth control was wrong." Indeed. Also for centuries, the Roman Catholic model of clerical celibacy predominated in Western Christendom. I hold both dogmas in low esteem, rejecting them as unscriptural teachings that fail to recognize the intrinsic, God-given worth of sexual relations between husband and wife. Mrs. Maken goes on to conflate singleness and birth control with obvious social evils such as divorce, abortion, and sexual immorality; it's simply guilt by association. If Mrs. Maken has a problem with birth control, as she seems to suggest, she needs to take her case to her compatriot Albert Mohler, who has stated that "evangelical couples may, at times, choose to use contraceptives in order to plan their families and enjoy the pleasures of the marital bed."[5] Perhaps Mrs. Maken should also realize that the very same culture that was for so long critical of birth control also looked down on a woman openly celebrating her own sexuality to the extent that Mrs. Maken does at end of her book. On page 189 she states, "I love the freedom to have legitimate sex whenever we want." The blue-haired ladies of days gone by would blush at such a frank remark.

A Cloud of Witnesses That Rains on Mrs. Maken's Parade

At any rate, how far back does Mrs. Maken want to go through the annals of Christendom to find support for her radical message of mandatory marriage for most everyone? Certainly, she would not want to go back to the writings of the Church Fathers. John Chrysostom, Gregory of Nyssa, Jerome, Athanasius, and Augustine are a few notables that come to mind who would be an embarrassment to her. These men went so far as to declare that virginity was spiritually superior to marriage (a position that not even I would defend).[6]

In chapter 4, Mrs. Maken states, "We must not assume that we understand singleness better than Christian thinkers of the past" (p. 74). What if the Reformers heeded this adage? Of course, if the great thinkers of the past paid obeisance to church hierarchy, historical tradition, and religious consensus the way many modern Evangelicals do, I suppose Protestantism would have never come about in the first place. Perhaps it's high time that some Christians write out ninety-five talking points on some sticky pads and affix them to the foreheads of some prominent religious leaders. All in all, Mrs. Maken commits the fallacy of "Appeal to Authority" in chapter 3. She fails to make a biblical case for her beliefs in first two chapters, so the reference to what religious authorities have thought about singleness and marriage in the past is gratuitous at best.

Whose Faith Anyway?

I believe in what some might call "soul competency." That is, the faith of my family or my church cannot save me, per se. It boils down to my personal relationship with Jesus Christ. In light of this, what religious authorities have to say about a question is no more meaningful than the opinion of Joe Normal if their doctrine is unscriptural. Their words are not what is going to judge me on the Final Day. Mrs. Maken may adhere to the Westminster Confession. I adhere to the Word of God. Let us never be afraid of reexamining the beliefs of those who have gone before. Let us base our faith on what the Holy Spirit clearly reveals in his written revelation, not on the ignorance and religiously motivated bigotry of our cultural forebears.

PART V

Chapter 4
"The Lack of Male Leadership: The True Cause of Protracted Singleness"
(Methinks the Lady Doth Protest Too Much)

As a man, I believe chapter 4 of Debbie Maken's book, *Getting Serious about Getting Married,* represents what is probably the lowest point of her narrative. Others have noted with concern the degree of animosity directed towards single men in Mrs. Maken's book, and I must share in this concern. I would have expected such animosity from a woman who is a feminist or, more generally, has no familiarity with the concept of biblical womanhood. That such animosity should come from a "Christian" writer favored by some notable religious figures, however, is alarming to say the least. This disturbing attitude is manifest throughout the book, but it is in chapter 4 where Mrs. Maken's anti-male sexism reaches its nadir.

Of Sitcoms and Men

Chapter 4 starts with a discussion of how single men are portrayed in popular media. Mrs. Maken complains, "Men are rarely pictured with wives and families (unless it's a mini-van commercial!). Instead, what's being sold is a life of fun and freedom; men are encouraged to pursue their own happiness and to extend their adolescence as long as possible" (p. 63). How does Mrs. Maken reach such a conclusion? She reaches it from considering sitcoms such as *Seinfeld*, *Friends*, and *Everybody Loves Raymond*. Personally, I cannot remember the last time I watched an episode of these negligible excuses for prime time programming, and I suspect the times I did catch a portion of these shows were due to unfortunate happenstance.

Seriously, are we to assume that our consumeristic, secularized media knows how to portray men in a favorable and accurate light? I invite readers to consider the scholarly research of Paul Nathanson and Katherine K. Young in their book, *Spreading Misandry: The Teaching of Contempt for Men in Popular Culture*.[1] I suspect that much, if not a majority, of the television programming available today manifests a pathologically demeaning view towards men. Women now represent a significant market share with respect to consumer goods and entertainment.[2] I am therefore not surprised that television, movies, etc. portray women as empowered and benevolent while portraying men as incompetent and diabolical.

Moreover, shall we consider how female irresponsibility is portrayed favorably in our popular media? What should we think of a culture that spawns such noteworthy works as *Thelma and Louise*, *Bridges of Madison County*, and *Sex and the City*? Surely, the whole female raunch culture (championed by the likes of Madonna) and the Girl Power movement has not escaped Mrs. Maken's attention. I am certain that Mrs. Maken would protest that most religious women she knows are not like the disreputable women we see in society at large. Just the same, the attitude of female entitlement in our culture manifests itself in subtle ways. I do not believe the sex who was deceived in the Garden of Eden is somehow less immune to the worldly messages of our popular culture than my own sex. If Mrs. Maken believes that Christian men are guilty of harkening to the cultural siren song of irresponsibility and narcissism, then she must acknowledge the same for Christian women.

Debbie Maken's Experiences vs. Objectivity

Continuing on page 64, Mrs. Maken says, "Most of the men I observed on the dating scene were essentially boys in men's clothing." What are we to make of such a statement? Are we to believe that Mrs. Maken's personal experiences represent an authoritative understanding of eligible men? Many men are rightfully frustrated and downright annoyed when women complain about there "being no good men left." When Debbie Maken makes acerbic remarks about dating "frogs who refused to become princes" and "boys in men's clothing," we must remember that we are considering the personal viewpoint of one woman. Her book does not relate the perspectives of the men she interacted with in her single years. What would these men tell us about Mrs. Maken? Would our impression of who she is change? I do not mean to impugn the character of Mrs. Maken, but her personal judgments must be placed in proper context.

What Feminism?

The section of chapter 4 that I find particularly disturbing is the one under the heading "The Bogey of Feminism." Sadly, it is here that Mrs. Maken evinces an attitude that is brazenly insensitive to the issues that effect men today. Our society has become notably hostile to men (a fact well understood by conservative commentators and various experts). Government, education, commerce, and popular culture have spat in the faces of men and boys. Now, regrettably even some religious leaders seem to have taken up the sport of male bashing. Feminism is squarely to blame for this sad turn of events, and more generally to blame for the breakdown of relationships between men and women.

"The Lack of Male Leadership: The True Cause of Protracted Singleness"

Mrs. Maken states, "The argument against Feminism goes like this: Feminists produced easy sex, and therefore marriages aren't happening now .... When we point to Feminism as the cause for singleness, we show our own hypocrisy. If indeed easy sex has deterred single men from marriage, then we need to concede that today's Christian single man is not celibate but is probably a sexually satisfied single" (p. 66). This disparaging remark against Christian single men overlooks one consideration: higher status males have more access to women than lower status males. Before the Sexual Revolution, monogamy insured that most men were guaranteed reliable access to the opposite sex. Now, on the heels of feminism, women celebrate their economic independence from men and champion their freedom from the restraints of traditional mores. They freely give their bodies away—but only to men of a certain calibre. Power excites women. Drug dealers, hooligans, rock stars, corporate executives, and ambitious pastors of megachurches do not go without female attention. In short, women are "going after the bad boys" and the "hot shots." Meanwhile, the "nice guys" get ignored. When women have been burned enough times by their taste in aggressive men, then they settle for more socially responsible men in their later years. There are plenty of nominally "Christian" women who have defrauded men in this regard. My readers should consider Angela Fiori's excellent essay, "To Single Men on Today's Women: Caveat Emptor." It includes a rather striking quote from a church leader:

> I've been in the ministry for 20 years and can tell you that pursuing jerks is definitely alive and well even among evangelical Christian women. They marry outside the faith about 6 times the rate of men because they think it's their will (not God's) to not only civilize the men but convert them to Christianity as well. No amount of reasoning will sway them. The end result is yet more broken families that the church has to take care of. Hence most 30s Christian singles classes are composed of 5–7 never-been-married men and 15 divorced women, a complete incompatibility. The women usually end up leaving after I point out that the New Testament (Matt 19:9, 1 Cor 7:10–11) forbids re-marriage for anyone divorced for a reason other than adultery and state that I have every intention of honoring this command. The wonderful result is that they burden liberal churches with the fallout of their past misadventures while I'm able to use my limited resources to preach the Word of God to people who are really interested in what it says.[3]

In essence, we should in keep mind that many women have no right to complain about the low quality of the men they date. All too often, these women either subconsciously or studiously avoid men of integrity because such men are deemed to be "too nice," "too boring," "not confident enough," "not ambitious," etc. These women need to take responsibility for their emotional immaturity and bad choices in life, instead of entertaining self-indulgent diatribes about how bad men are.

Female promiscuity, however, is not the only thing for which we can blame feminism. It is feminism that pushed no-fault divorce, and now we find it is mostly women who initiate these type of divorces.[4] Many hold their children for ransom from the fathers and financially ruin their ex-husbands with draconian court settlements. It is feminism that pushed for the VAWA, and now we have men being handcuffed and taken from their homes on the most dubious grounds of spousal abuse. Meanwhile, society is largely indifferent to the empirical findings about how women abuse men at roughly the same level as men do women.[5] It is feminism that demanded changes to our educational system, and now we have an educational environment that is hostile to boys. Boys are lagging behind girls in public schools, but strangely enough, are doing just fine when they are home-schooled.[6] It is feminism that demanded changes to the workplace, and now a qualified male applicant for job can be passed up for a less qualified female applicant in the name of affirmative action.

Everywhere we look, we see women who sexually abuse minors getting a slap on wrist, whereas the same act by a man would most certainly guarantee him a lengthy prison sentence. The abuse of women by men is regarded as an outrage; the opposite is fodder for romantic comedies. Women who murder their children and husbands are presumed to have been the victim of some abuse or mental disorder, but the same act by a man earns him the label of "monster." All this because women refuse to hold other women accountable, and because too many men, in their warped notion of chivalry, come to the defense of dishonorable women.

Mrs. Maken opines that blaming feminist theory "is as untenable as pretending Adam's silence and lack of leadership had nothing to do with fall" (p. 66). In making such a bald assertion, Mrs. Maken ignores one point: God punished Eve—right after he punished the Serpent. Eve was held accountable. If there was a failure on Adam's part, it is that he did not hold Eve accountable, but instead deferred to her faulty judgment. It is our failure today. We need to stop automatically deferring to women, and start holding them accountable for their actions. Mrs. Maken and women like her may have tasted the fruit of gynocentrism, but men like me are not biting what she offers.

The Self-Deception of Conservative Women

Mrs. Maken would have us believe that women are entirely passive agents in the sorry state of affairs that confronts both sexes today. In this respect, I see very little difference between Mrs. Maken's attitude and the worldview of feminists who constantly portray women as victims and men as oppressors.

The insistence of Mrs. Maken and other women that they are rendered helpless because it is men who supposedly initiate relationships is profoundly disingenuous. Often it is the female who signals receptivity to the men in which she is interested, and it is the female with either accepts or rejects the advances of men.[7]

We must also consider those situations where women practice a type of preemptive selectivity by letting men know up front what their mating preferences are. In the online dating world, for example, profiles of women (religious or otherwise) mention a laundry list of demands with which men must comply before a response to said men is even deemed worthwhile (e.g., physical requirements, educational requirements, monetary requirements, etc.). Women are not pieces of fruit hanging on a tree, haplessly plucked by whatever man takes the initiative to reach forth his hand. No, they share in the responsibility for their protracted singleness. Their own demeanor, mating preferences, etc. are much a determining factor in their marital status as any chance male that comes across them.

Perhaps where conservative women have become rather selective is in presuming that having husbands who make more money than them is a birthright. Consider author Willard Harley's description of the type of man that women supposedly find "irresistible": "He assumes the responsibility to house, feed, and clothe the family. If his income is insufficient to provide essential support, he resolves the problem by upgrading his skills to increase his salary. He does not work long hours, keeping himself from his wife and family, but is able to provide necessary support by working a forty to forty-five-hour week. While he encourages his wife to pursue a career, he does not depend on her salary for family living expenses."[8] How should we respond to this quote by a relationship expert renowned among many Evangelicals? Do religious women demand the right to have exciting careers in order to make some discretionary income, and yet expect men to "exercise biblical leadership" by making a larger paycheck than them?

Apparently, the concept of the Tragedy of the Commons is lost on said women. They do not understand the cumulative effect of women competing with men for money, status, and power in our society. It means there are less desirable men for women with hypergamous tendencies (i.e., those women who want to "marry up"). For every woman that takes a man's job, there is a man who is denied an income that he could have used to support a woman. It is a simple and undeniable fact. Mrs. Maken remarks: "We think women today deserve to be single for choices they made, like attending college or buying a house. How dare they be successful and leave men behind? As if one sex's success prevents the other's" (p. 67). All the same, we cannot indulge a fairy-tale view of economics where scarcity does not exist, where good-paying jobs are not limited by market forces, where the social pyramid isn't pathetically small at the top, or where the middle class isn't shrinking.

The wedges of the pie can only be sliced so thin in order for everyone to have a bite.

We should not be surprised when an educated woman has difficulty finding a mate with a similar or higher level of education and earning potential. Men, for the most part, do not look at potential spouses the way women do. Often, a woman's social status is not as important to men as the woman's physical and emotional attractiveness. As long as a woman is reasonably attractive and well-mannered, men are going to pay attention to her. I'll be candid here: I think many men are much more realistic about the standards they set for women than vice versa. If a woman wants to compete with men in the most lucrative of careers, and yet insist on finding a husband who has achieved more than her, I grant her that prerogative. If the proverbial prince doesn't show up with the glass slipper, however, then she cannot blame men for the consequences of her own discriminating tastes.

Adam Made Me Do It

On pages 67 and 68, we read the following from Mrs. Maken:

> I have heard people in the church say that when women take the lead, men retreat, pointing to Genesis and the actions of Eve. We have it backwards. When men sit in silence and forgo leadership, women start doing things. Adam was in the garden with Eve, had been given headship over her, watched the entire conversation (with a talking snake!), and yet did nothing. No intervention, no "Stop talking with that animal!" It's like he sat back, popped open a beer, and then when everything went to pot complained, "The woman you gave me ..."

> ... Just because women have careers in virtually every field does not mean they want the independence of being single. Women often have no choice but to prepare themselves to be market competitors because they cannot rely upon men to marry them, or for that matter to stay married to them.

I must admit that I find Mrs. Maken's retelling of the Genesis account rather imaginative. Just the same, God did not say to Adam, "Because you didn't stop your wife from eating ..." Rather, he punished Adam for "listening" to his wife and taking the fruit she offered him. As for Eve, she could not make the kind of excuses many women make today and say to God, "If Adam had been a more responsible husband, I wouldn't have done this." Excuse-making is no more the prerogative of the distaff gender than it is of those who are "called to lead."

Mrs. Maken's exoneration of career women is nothing short of a cop-out. Why do women have to compete in the job market with men? They could

"The Lack of Male Leadership: The True Cause of Protracted Singleness"

stay under their parent's roof until they are married. If financial necessity compels them to work, why is it necessary for them to seek the most lucrative and prestigious of jobs traditionally held by men? If they feel their aptitudes are best put to use in a prestigious career, why must they then backpedal on gender roles and expect the men they marry to be the primary or sole breadwinners? Finally, I find it strange that women are insecure about failed marriages when they, as I have indicated, initiate most of the no-fault divorces and drain their ex-husbands' bank accounts. Indeed, how do we explain the phenomenon of husband hopping? Thanks to the Divorce Industry, many women have done quite well financially.

Stranger still is Mrs. Maken's about face in declaring that we should praise women for their educational accomplishments anyway. She says on page 68, "We mistakenly think that if a woman has her affairs in order, she's sending off signs of independence. We vilify her instead of complimenting her for industriousness and intelligence." She goes into detail about how educated women are valued in Eastern countries like India (implying that we in the West should have the same attitude). I am frankly puzzled. In one place, we have some reference to Adam's laziness and how women are forced to work, and in another, we are supposed to be holding up "educated" women as prize catches. Let's be honest: women do not get advanced technical degrees in order to do housework. They get degrees because they covet the same high-paying jobs as men do. Either the presence of women in the workforce is a good thing or it isn't. If it is a good thing, then we should stop blaming men if they don't do anything about it. If it is not a good thing, then we should stop praising women who are pursuing prestigious careers.

As if Mrs. Maken's logic wasn't weird enough, we have this statement at the end of page 68: "Most men interviewed on this subject today say they prefer independent women who can carry their own weight. Men, in general, do not want women to be dependent ... This proves that most men today want a 'pay your own way' type of deal where the mantle of adult responsibilities of assuming the care of another is avoided and their personal autonomy remains unchecked. This allows many men to keep jobs that resemble hobbies and to maintain hobbies as costly as their jobs." Yes, you read that. First, career women are victims of male passivity. Yet, they are supposed to be praised as a prize catch like they are in India. Now, men are immature sloths for wanting the very women that Mrs. Maken says are a prize catch. Confused? I don't blame you.

It seems that many contemporary women suffer from a bout of collective amnesia. They feel oppressed because they cannot easily opt out of the drudgery of the workplace and stay at home with the children they love. They want to blame men for their woeful lot. How quickly they forget that it was mostly women who brought about this situation. Women can thank the feminists for despising motherhood, for demanding that women be able to compete in the marketplace with men, etc. Men did not wake up one day and put a gun to the heads of their wives and tell them to get to work. Mrs. Maken forgets the cries of "male chauvinist pigs," "female oppression," "desperate housewives" and "equality." Just what does Mrs. Maken propose men should do? Should we take away the political and economic rights of women? Shall we force women into a subservient position?

Yes, it is true that many men *currently* prefer educated women who can take care of themselves. I am certain this was not always the case. We forget that the *willing* entrance of women into the workforce has probably created an employer's market as far as jobs are concerned. Wages have stagnated, and good paying jobs have been outsourced. Now, the proverbial genie is out of the bottle and it usually takes two incomes for most families to get by. It is no wonder then that men want wives who are willing to work outside the home. We should not assume from this that men find this to be an ideal situation, nor should we think most men are avoiding "the mantle of adult responsibilities of assuming the care of another" as Mrs. Maken avers (Ibid.). Indeed, if we equate the size of one's income with "the care of another," are we to infer from Mrs. Maken that women are entitled to not care very much about their husbands? I remind my readers that in the original Greek language, the subject of 1 Timothy 5:8 is neutral in gender and applies to both women and men.

Mrs. Maken and so many women have put the cart before the horse. Women will say that they can't follow if men won't lead, but the truth lies in the converse. Remember the saying, "You can lead a horse to water but you can't make it drink"? Conservative women blame men for not sticking a feeding tube down the horses mouth, or balk at us if we actually try. No matter what happens, men are blamed. However, we need to stop blaming men just because women are collectively reaping what they have sown. When it comes to choosing between traditional gender roles and modernity, too many women want to have their cake and eat it, too. In the process, they are choking themselves on the dough. If a woman wants a man to "lead," then she needs to get out of the driver's seat.

The Princes of Zoan

On page 70, Mrs. Maken makes the following statement: "... because we have an unprecedented number of people entering college, there is a race to the top, where people feel the need to pursue an unprecedented number of post-graduate degrees to distinguish themselves from what is now considered the average." Should we be surprised? Generations ago, a man could support an entire family on a job that required no more than a high-school education. Now with the onslaught of women entering the workforce, automation, and jobs being outsourced to third-world countries with pathetic labor practices, people most certainly have to "distinguish themselves" in order to survive. It

"The Lack of Male Leadership: The True Cause of Protracted Singleness"

is high time that some pundits who want to blame men for the problems we face wake up and smell the coffee.

For too long in our society, we have taken ordinary men for granted. We have declared them obsolete. We have taxed them into destitution so that we may fund the very programs that we think will replace the need for men. Corporations, in their greed, have turned their back on working men and joined in "a race to the bottom." They make themselves out to be the fair winners in a game of "free enterprise," forgetting how much they have benefitted from government despotism and corruption. Religious leaders have been strangely silent on these issues; too many of them seem to pay homage to the wealthy and powerful in our society instead of heeding the cries of the oppressed. Do we think that God is indifferent to this turn of events?

There was a time when a family was responsible for its own food, clothing, shelter, education of youth, etc. Now, as a society, we have placed our trust in the captains of government and commerce to make our lives better. In Isaiah, chapter 30, God condemned Israel for wrongfully trusting in Egypt for deliverance. In a similar fashion, a day of reckoning nears for many. Can our Egyptian princes of Zoan save us? Our government is infested with lackeys sold out to highest bidder. Commerce is run by the smugly indifferent who make their fortunes off the blood, sweat, and tears of the faceless throng.

Let's stop sermonizing about what average men should be doing. We are hypocrites in that we have utterly betrayed them. We have sold them down the river. We were so busy shaming men, belittling them with our sermons about the Saturday night sins of the working class. We nagged them about their sexual fantasies, their drinking, their yelling at their wives, etc. Meanwhile, the high places of consumerism, careerism, avarice, selfish ambition, bigotry, prejudice, authoritarianism, and misandry went unassailed.

We have talked a good talk about the need for "strong families" and yet failed to give help to the very bedrock of a strong family—the man. What "help" was given was little more than finger-wagging and demands that men be held accountable (viz., the PromiseKeepers movement). Mrs. Maken's book is just more of the same. Let our pundits go down to Egypt—to the ones in which they trusted. Can the government fund a program for Christian women to have children? Can commerce shrink-wrap strong families and place them on the shelves at Wal-Mart? Will our religious pundits start "outreach ministries" to provide husbands to lonely Christian bachelorettes? In short, the pundits who talk about "strong families" and yet refuse to appreciate the problems that plague ordinary men are akin to Rahab-Hem-Shebeth (Isa. 30:1–7).

Dysfunctional Families - Immature Adults?

Near the end of chapter 4, Mrs. Maken points to the failure of modern families to help young people transition to adulthood. I actually find myself agreeing with several of the points she makes on pages 71–73, but naturally, I have my reservations as well. One problem is that Mrs. Maken understands marriage and family as a necessary transition to adulthood for most people. I understand why some see marriage and family as necessary for chastity, happiness, church memberships, and a healthy economy (although I disagree with that mindset). However, if marriage is necessary for adulthood as well, then are we to believe the Apostle Paul was an immature man? Surely not.

I think we need to back away from the assumption that marriage and family are rites of passage into adulthood, per se. In fact, my recommendation for single people is that they complete their rite of passage into adulthood *before* they get married. The world is already full of immature spouses and parents who married in haste and, all too often, end up repenting in leisure. Our social landscape is strewn with wrecked households that do not give glory to God. In this regard, the doctrines taught by Debbie Maken and those akin to her do not help.

Their Young Women Had No "Unchained Melody"

There is another matter that perturbs me about Mrs. Maken's discussion of dysfunctional homes and parental failure. She addresses these matters in a chapter discussing the "lack of male leadership." Excuse me for pointing out the obvious, but women come from dysfunctional homes, too. Is it possible that many women have not been properly trained by their parents to assume the mantle of biblical womanhood?

Debbie Maken quotes Psalms 78:63 on page 11, "Their young women had no marriage song." I think the reason many young women have no "marriage song" is that they have been too busy playing Cyndi Lauper's ditty, "Girls Just Want to Have Fun" on their iPods. Indeed, Mrs. Maken admits on page 11: "When I was in my early twenties, I didn't really mind being single; after, my life was full." Camerin Courtney echoes Mr. Mrs. Maken's sentiments in a recent online article: "Maken starts with a relatable description of many single women's experience: Singleness is easier to see as a grand adventure in your 20s, an unfettered time to figure out who you are and what path God might like you to take through life. Without a spouse, there's more freedom to travel and take risks, minister and invest in a burgeoning career."[9] How revealing these sentiments are. I suppose for many young women, male companionship seems unnecessary and perhaps an imposition. However, as women get older and their biological clocks start ticking, they expect men to start paying attention to them. Why weren't the suitors of yesteryear not good enough?

"The Lack of Male Leadership: The True Cause of Protracted Singleness"

If women believe that marriage is a necessity, then why aren't they preparing for it in their younger years? As it is, what messages about womanhood do we think girls receive from our popular media? Instead of seeing boys as the ones they will marry one day, they see T-Shirts that say, "Boys are stupid. Throw rocks at them." Instead of seeing women that extend courtesy and respect to the men in their lives, they see women who insult their fathers, brothers, and husbands. Instead of seeing women who take pride in motherhood and being "keepers of the home," they are told to find their fulfillment in the workplace. Instead of learning to compromise in human relationships, they are told to be aggressive and settle for nothing less than what they want. Instead of learning the value of objective truth, they are taught that their feelings are more important than what others think. Instead of embracing the accountabilty that comes with being a grown woman, they are taught to see themselves as "victims of the Patriarchy." Instead of seeing themselves as helpmates for men, they are taught to see themselves as competitors against men. Men are seen as tools to be used, as obstacles to overcome, or even as enemies to vanquish, but not as human beings to be loved. There has been a failure to correct these negative trends among our young women. Why aren't our families doing more about this situation?

Therefore, many women, religious or otherwise, should not marvel at why men seem hesitant to approach them. Men are increasingly eschewing those women who are insulting, condescending, ill-mannered, quarrelsome, materialistic, disloyal, treacherous, vindictive, petty, sanctimonious, autocratic, demanding, self-centered, and "the such like." The coarsening of womanhood in our culture is pandemic. No wonder, then, that some men have sought out foreign women to be their brides. Many men do not want to keep a woman "barefoot and pregnant"; they just want be valued, cherished, and respected . Unfortunately, for a lot of contemporary women in our culture, even this seems to be asking too much.

Dysfunctional Churches

I have to agree with Mrs. Maken when she claims that churches have failed singles. Of course, I believe the failure lies in something other than what Mrs. Maken holds to be the case. Churches have failed singles by propping up marriage as some means of sanctification that most people must undergo. Churches have failed singles by treating them as less than complete human beings. Mrs. Maken's teachings represent more of the same failure.

On pages 74–75, Mrs. Maken wants churches to stand up for the truth on the matter. Unfortunately, as I have stated in my earlier remarks on Mrs. Maken's book, her teachings are not scriptural. If churches insist on pushing Mrs. Maken's hobby, they should be prepared for a fight. I do not doubt that congregations can be split, families fractured, and people turned off from a church over the radical pro-marriage agenda of some teachers. Of course, these teachers, who have a zeal without knowledge, will mistake their factiousness for the will of God. That is why those of us who oppose their harmful teachings must be ready to contend earnestly for the faith (Jude 3), and stand like Paul did against the Judaizers, not yielding "even for an hour" (Gal. 2:1–5).

Mrs. Maken states, "The church has no obligation to match-make or start a dating service" (p. 74). Really? If marriage is such a necessary component of the human condition for most people, then a church would most certainly need to be involved. I remind my readers that one of the functions of a church is to provide benevolence to believers (James 2:15–16; 1 Tim. 5:16; 1 Cor. 16:1–3). In other words, it is to make sure that those believers who are not able to obtain the necessities of life for themselves are given what they need. A church is also to help believers to fulfill whatever individual responsibilities they have as Christians if they are not able to do so by themselves (1 Cor. 12:12–26; Gal. 6:2). So, for instance, if a believer does not have transportation to the church building, the congregation needs to provide it so the believer doesn't end up forsaking the assembly. In short, Mrs. Maken can't have it both ways. She can't rank sexual companionship among the basic necessities of life and yet say a church is not responsible for those who are unable to lawfully provide for themselves in this matter.

Mrs. Maken meekly grants that "it would not be unbiblical for a church to assist in this manner as examples of past Christian charities have proved. Having accountability groups for single men to examine their perennial singleness is on par with having accountability groups for other issues that trouble us" (p. 75). So her idea of being charitable is holding men accountable for something over which they may or may not have control. It's more finger-wagging once again, providing no substantive help to those men that face stiff social obstacles to getting married. Frankly, the word "accountability group" raises a red flag in my mind. I understand that a church can be a place where people foster trusting relationships and share struggles with fellow brothers and sisters in the faith. The manufactured, micromanaged confessions of some "accountability groups," however, smacks of an authoritarian, and cultish behavior that is out of harmony with what the Bible teaches (1 Peter 4:15; Matt. 20:25–28). A person who has never married simply does not need to give an account for his marital status to his religious leaders. As it is, Mrs. Maken's words are soothing in the ears of religious leaders who, like the Pharisees, want to bind heavy burdens on people but not lift one finger to help (Matt. 23:4).

I also want to say that I sense a great deal of complacency among religious leaders. They and their followers have turned inward, insulating themselves from a world that is dying to hear the Gospel. Many churches want to complain about cultural issues, but they do not want to step outside their social comfort zones and minister to those who have never darkened the door of a place where Christians assemble. Expanding the borders of the Kingdom of God is just too inconvenient for some in this regard. So, many religious leaders rely on second-generation or third-generation believers to fill their pews. We are so fond of claiming that "God has no grandchildren" but we throw this saying right out the window when a discussion of marriage or church growth comes up. Mrs. Maken's teaching may provide some comfort to church leaders who see their membership rolls grow shorter and the hairs of their congregants grow grayer with each passing year. Perhaps church leaders think if they throw out a few false platitudes as Mrs. Maken does, the young couples in their midst will procreate and empty pews will be filled again. Perhaps they think they can secure a fresh supply of young, impressionable minds to catechize with their "commandments of men" (Mark 7:7). Is God impressed with this?

Church leaders may proclaim that "strong families" are the backbone of the Lord's Church, but they are wrong. *Faithful Christians* are the backbone of the Lord's Church. Faithful Christians may or may not have grown up in a religious household. It doesn't matter. Their obedience to the Lord is what matters (Matt. 12:48–50). As I have indicated in earlier remarks about Mrs. Maken's book, the Kingdom of God grows by spiritual means, not physical means (Mark 4:30–32; Matt. 28:18–20; 1 Peter 1:22–23). All must come to Christ by the same way: obeying his Gospel (2 Thess. 1:8). Therefore the question of making babies to help the Church is moot.

In a discussion about marriage and children, many commentators like to talk about "norms" in the Biblical record. Of course, some "norms" are culturally incidental and are not binding on Christians today (e.g., foot-washing). Yet, if we want to talk about "norms," why isn't anyone considering the New Testament "norm" for church growth—evangelism? We think having new families in order to spur church growth is par for the course. We should, in fact, regard such as scandalous. When we claim that families are the lifeblood of churches, we are saying that the Gospel has no effect on the lives of people and that religious conviction is merely a matter of cultural conditioning at an early age.

Perhaps some churches actually deserve to have their numbers dwindle and disappear. They have "forsaken their first love" like the Ephesians in the book of Revelation. Some of them are so politicized and held captive to their culturally-bound understanding of Christianity that they have ended up preaching a false social gospel of either the left-wing or right-wing variety. I say all of these things to make this point: Religious leaders should stop goading single men to "be fruitful and multiply" in order to fill pews. These leaders need to repent of pushing a distorted, fleshly view of Christianity and came back to the plain truths of the Gospel. If they sow according to the truth, then God will give them the increase, numerically and/or spiritually (John 15:1–8). Otherwise, "let the dead bury the dead."

One Tune Not Playing on Mrs. Maken's Jukebox

Finally, let me note that a recent study showed that men were more interested in marriage than women. Even among fundamentalist Protestants, 68.4% of the males studied favored marriage compared to 59.3% of the females.[10] This revelation stands as an indictment of essentially everything Mrs. Maken says about men in her book. Her fanciful notion of "boys in men's clothing" is a canard. I think it's high time we stop asking what's wrong with men and start asking ourselves what external forces discourage them from marrying. On page 65, Mrs. Maken says, "Don't get me wrong—I like men. I even married one." I do not doubt that Mrs. Maken "likes" men in that she is sexually attracted to them. The question, however, is whether or not she *respects* them. Sadly after reading chapter 4 of her book, I have difficulty seeing how such is the case.

PART VI

Chapter 5
"What We've Been Taught"
(Debbie Maken's Bone to Pick)

On page 79 of *Getting Serious about Getting Married*, Mrs. Maken raises a hypothetical situation where a woman who is starving to death shows up at a church. Mrs. Maken asks her readers what would be an appropriate response by the church to this woman. Naturally, most readers would agree with Mrs. Maken's answer: "The last thing we'd say is, 'Man shall not live by bread alone, but by every word that comes from the mouth of God.'" People would recognize that the woman's physical needs must be met as well as her spiritual needs. However, Mrs. Maken claims the same holds true for a person's desire to marry. We are told that an emphasis on spiritual growth is no substitute in this regard.

With such an understanding in mind, Mrs. Maken spends the following chapters lambasting much of the spiritual advice church leaders give to single people (e.g., how singles can be content in their situation). Her understanding, of course, is flawed. Sex and companionship is not parallel to the basic biological urges of eating, sleeping, etc. Indeed, we have to ask why God has placed so many restrictions on the sexual drive and why he demands moral accountability with regard to our romantic desires. Where there is moral accountability, there must be the power to choose between good and evil. As it is, people do not die from the lack of sex, and there is no innate need for people to get married.

Chapter 5 rehashes claims made earlier in Mrs. Maken's book: men are responsible for pursuing marriage, God only allows a few people to be single, etc. I have already addressed these claims in my critique. Granted, in the pages that follow chapter 5, Mrs. Maken raises some legitimate issues. I agree with her about how some religious pundits have unnecessarily frustrated single people. Many church leaders presume too much when they think God wants certain individuals to settle for singleness. Having said that, Mrs. Maken's attempt to grapple with the frustrations that single people face is undercut by her own short-sighted conclusions in the first four chapters of her book. In the following sections of my critique, I plan to address some of

Mrs. Maken's concerns about how churches treat single people. There is still much about her book that I find to be disappointing at best.

PART VII

Chapter 6
"The 'Gift' of Singleness and the Sovereignty of God"
(Magic 8-Balls and the Present Distress about Presents)

How does God operate in the lives of believers? Does he have a special mate picked out for every one of us? These are tantalizing questions and I suspect that they have been the fodder for a lot of theological speculation (or should I say "whittling on God's end of the stick"). In light of these kind of questions, Mrs. Maken devotes chapter 6 of her book to a discussion about how people relate the sovereignty of God to their chances of getting married. I must admit that Mrs. Maken raises some legitimate issues about the assumptions many people have about God's providence. However, as I have indicated, Mrs. Maken application of her principles still leaves something to be desired.

On page 86, Mrs. Maken attests to the sovereignty of God while upholding the responsibility of human beings. We are not mindless, passive agents directed by the Creator, but must cooperate with what God has planned for us. To this sentiment, I say a hearty "Amen." I have to concede that if a person wants to get married but simply waits for God to send some sort of mysterious sign about what direction to take in finding a spouse, success probably won't follow. Moreover, even in the promises that God has clearly made to his children, faith requires obedience. It was true under the Old Testament; it is true today.

Mrs. Maken, however, then asks a question at the bottom of page 87: "If singleness is a gift like marriage, and if the two are both morally equal and good, then why pursue marriage?" I understand that Mrs. Maken probably meant this to be a rhetorical question, but I thought I turn it back on Mrs. Maken and her supporters. Truly, why would anyone want to trade the benefits of singleness for marriage? There must be an answer to this question that doesn't involve the misapplication of scriptures, dubious studies that don't distinguish between correlation and causality, sanctimonious platitudes about how adversity builds character, or language that is downright insulting.

One Woman's Refuse is Another Man's Gift

Mrs. Maken, naturally, does not see singleness as a gift. She assumes that calling singleness a gift is a *"non sequitur."* We are told that since God only called a select few to be single and enabled them through the "gift of celibacy," we cannot logically assume that just anyone should be content to be single. Of course, I reject Mrs. Maken's assumptions about the "gift of celibacy" as they are based on flimsy conjecture about what Paul teaches in 1 Corinthians 7.

Mrs. Maken asks a lot of rhetorical questions about singleness as a gift. Why do so many people hate being single? Why are they single for so long? Why weren't there more singles in the past? What happened to the Genesis mandate to "be fruitful and multiply"? Why have so many singles lost their virginity? I have dealt with the so-called "mandate" of Genesis in my earlier comments. As for the other questions, they make for some interesting talking points but they establish nothing substantive in a case for marriage.

In fact, I could turn around and ask those who think marriage is a gift why so many people want to divorce. Why are so many marriages unhappy? Why is there an entire cottage industry devoted to churning out books about how to bring excitement into lackluster relationships? Why do I see so many husband and wives who look stressed out, jaded, tired, and unenthusiastic about their situation? Is marriage is gift to these people? I do not need a miraculous gift of asexuality to understand that marriage often does not bring the happiness that many people think it will. Gifts, like beauty, are often in the eye of the beholder.

Biblical Thinking Vs. Outcome-Based Theology

Debbie Maken makes some interesting remarks on pages 88–90:

> Thinking culturally endorses a seductive, outcome-based theology: Whatever your outcome is—whether you are married or single—it must be God's will. But God is not a puppet, and we should not treat him as a such. We must not turn his sovereignty and his will into *carte blanche* approval for the choices we make. Doing so turns the doctrine of God's sovereignty (his control in exercising his will) into a rubber-stamping machine that validates every situation in life, no matter how unbiblical or personally devastating.

This is wonderful advice to heed. Just the same, I wonder how Mrs. Maken reconciles her exegetical principles with her statement on page 15: "... I was never going to get true spiritual peace about singleness because I wasn't called to singleness, and the Spirit does not give peace about something that is outside of God's calling." Somehow we are to believe that Debbie Maken's discontentment with singleness was a sign from God that she was to be married. Somehow we are to believe that failure of people to remain chaste is a sign that marriage is a requisite for them as well. Moreover, we see throughout Mrs. Maken's book sentiments that are often expressed in popular culture: people cannot live without sex, romance is the key to happiness, unmarried men are pathetic, men need to be ambitious and make money in order to be good husbands, men are to blame for the problems women face, etc.

Who are we to say that Debbie Maken isn't engaging in a little bit of outcome-based theology herself? Perhaps she is the one who is guilty of "thinking culturally." Mrs. Maken should have been more careful about the kind of charges she levels against others in the matter of theology. The measure she uses has been measured against her, and she is found wanting.

Really, is it any wonder that Mrs. Maken's exegesis is flawed? On page 90, she misapplies 1 Corinthians 7:1–2 to single people whereas the original language, grammar, and context show that the Apostle Paul was addressing married people. On page 92, she uses the reference to the "wife" of one's "youth" in Malachi 2:15 as a proof-text for demanding that people get married young. Of course, that is not the focus of Malachi of 2:15 and such a reading puts us in the absurd position of barring marriage to anyone over the age of 35. All in all, I believe Mrs. Maken's misunderstanding of what the Bible teaches may very well be the result of her attempt to superimpose her own cultural values on the Scriptures—a case of her failing to follow her own advice.

The Sovereignty of God and the Problem of Evil (or Singleness)

Debbie Maken is correct that singleness is a product of human free will. The fact that there so many unhappily single women is indeed the result of some choices made by individuals and by the culture at large. Mrs. Maken lists her favorite culprits: modern dating, the education system, failed families, immaturity, and of course, men. Noticeably absent from her list is corporatism, feminism, and the shallowness of many contemporary women. Mrs. Maken's narrative gingerly marches right along and summarily ignores the 300-pound gorillas in the room.

Yet Mrs. Maken is also correct that that God is not obligated to save people from the temporal consequences of their decisions. There is truly such a thing as "generational sin" in the sense that people often suffer the fallout of foolish choices made long beforehand by others. We therefore need to take a cue from Mrs. Maken and ask ourselves if the unhappiness of women today is the result of "generational sin."

As a case in point, women today are becoming dissatisfied with the passivity of men. Yet for one generation, we have shouted men down, told them that their masculinity is oppressive and problematic, claimed that they need to change, etc. Can we blame men when they are in many cases only a former husk of what they used to be? Let us consider another matter: women entering into midlife alone and single. What or who is the culprit? Is it men who are afraid to commit, or is it women who have insisted on frittering away their youth on careerism and frivolity?

What I am suggesting is that while Mrs. Maken is correct on some principles, she misses the mark in her application. Women are not only reaping the bitter consequences of choices made by others, they are reaping the consequences of their own self-centered, rash decisions. Even Mrs. Maken should be asking herself if her late marriage was really the fault of the society around her or a carefree attitude that she may have had in her younger years. I read her description of herself in her early twenties on page 11 and wonder if "getting serious about getting married" wasn't really a high priority for her at that time.

Let us turn from the matter of singleness for a moment and realize that even the choice of marrying has consequences. I pose this question: Suppose a woman is married to an emotionally indifferent man. He doesn't cheat on her, so she has no scriptural grounds for divorce (Matt. 19:9). Is it the will of God for this woman to be in a loveless marriage? I suggest that is no more appropriate to say it is the will of God that people should marry than it is to say he wants them to be single.

Why is this so? Simple. We have no business presuming to know the mind of our Creator on a matter if he has not clearly revealed such to us (Deut. 29:29). As it is, despite what Mrs. Maken would have us believe, there is no divine revelation that personally directs us to get married, per se. In the matter of matrimony, we can pray for wisdom and guidance, but the decision to marry is essentially a decision that God leaves to us. He no more tells us which specific person we should wed than he does which road we should take to the grocery mart. The "secret things belong to the Lord." It is our job to pray, trust, and obey, not to peer through the veil of the heavens the way some peer into a Magic 8-ball. In essence, chapter 6 leaves us with a valuable lesson about not assuming too much about the "will of God." Unfortunately, Mrs. Maken fails to heed her own advice.

PART VIII

Chapter 7
"'Wait on the Lord'"
(Act Now Before It's Too Late)

Chapter 7 of Debbie Maken's book is puzzling to me. We are asked on page 97, "Does God really seek indefinite waiting on the part of single women to get married? Does God really seek unlimited patience in waiting for Mr. Right to appear?" Mrs. Maken consequently spends the rest of the chapter exhorting her audience to be more proactive about marriage.

Wait on the Lord ... Or Wait on the Men?

Here's the ironic part: There is a doctrine, popular among Evangelicals, which equates initiation of romantic relationships with male leadership. Men must make the first move in a love affair according to this line of thinking. In order to give this doctrine legitimacy, many religious pundits scour the Old Testament for examples of how women and men should engage in courtship. Awkward situations like Ruth approaching Boaz are explained away in one fashion or another. Other passages like Proverbs 18:22 are given a secondary meaning. The saying that "whoever finds a wife finds favor with the Lord" is reinterpreted from a promise to a commandment that men must be the ones doing the finding. Like many commentators, Debbie Maken believes men must take the initiative in forming relationships with women. Hence we have a paradox. Debbie Maken doesn't want women to be passive about their situation, but her views on courtship demand just that.

I know that Mrs. Maken feels that women can be more proactive by doing such things as demanding "accountability" from men. However, many women already complain enough as it is about single men failing to commit. I don't see how more of the same is going to help the situation. A single woman may come up with some stratagems for getting men to become more serious about marriage, but that doesn't mean men will become more serious about *her*. Debbie Maken simply fails to give women any meaningful tools for encouraging men to approach them. At the end of the day, a single man may be more devoted to the cause of marriage and yet excuse his personal situation by simply noting that he "hasn't found the right one." I daresay that

Mrs. Maken and others could say nothing to him. Pious platitudes are one thing; individual application is another.

The High Cost of Waiting

In chapter 7, Mrs. Maken notes the costs that come with delaying marriage. These include decreased opportunities for childbearing, more years of sexual frustration and temptation, lost opportunities for shared experiences with a spouse, increased difficulty in changing behavioral patterns that develop while one is single, etc. We have to grant that these concerns are legitimate. However, these are also the high costs of a culture that encourages young women to embrace careerism over relationships. These are the high costs of women who, in their youth, spurn the advances of good men because of mating preferences that are too demanding. These are the costs of women believing what popular culture says about cheating time and "having it all."

Marriage in one's youth has its own costs, too. With youth comes immaturity, and with immaturity comes rash decisions that one may later regret. With younger marriages, the opportunities for certain experiences and self-discovery that come with a single lifestyle are lost forever. Many decisions in life of monumental importance have their own price tag. Mrs. Maken and those like her paint a misleading picture when they conveniently omit these costs from their tally sheet. If there were no costs to marrying young, the women of yesteryear would have never expressed feelings about being trapped, isolated, and oppressed in traditional marriages. People, but especially women in our culture, are going to have to learn that the proverbial grass is not greener on the other side. There is no perfect situation or lasting moments of transcendence this side of eternity. So much of life depends on one's attitude, not upon ideal circumstances.

The High Cost in Dollar Signs - Do We Really Want to Go There?

The other costs of singleness to which Debbie Maken draws attention are the economic and social costs of a dwindling population. Some would have us to be concerned about labor shortages, shortage of consumers, fewer taxpayers, smaller militaries, an increased strain on the Social Security system, etc. Yet as a fiscal conservative, I wonder why I should be worried about there being fewer taxpayers and consequently fewer dollars for a bloated government to funnel into the coffers of bureaucrats. I personally think the military-industrial complex and the welfare machine of the Nanny State could stand to be weaned. Furthermore, why should I be concerned about the market suddenly favoring laborers and buyers; let the captains of our "global economy," the monopolists, and the plutocrats trouble themselves about such matters. Why is there so much urgency to create more babies to promote the interests of the wealthy and powerful? Whose agenda are Mrs. Maken and those like her trying to protect?

I am very concerned when certain commentators who claim to uphold marriage and family betray a very utilitarian viewpoint toward other human beings, and I hope Mrs. Maken has no intention of leaning in that direction. Religious commentators may bemoan the prospect of marriage being seen as a private matter. Granted, in one sense marriage is not private. The married are accountable to God and cannot live without concern for others. Yet in another sense, marriage is private in that it is ordained for the good of the people who enter into it, not for any utility it might have for society. The marriage of a man and woman has worth endowed upon it by the Almighty. If we decry the commodification of sex through pornography, etc., then we must have the same protective attitude toward marriage. We must reject any mindset that would reduce marriage to a mere cog in the larger machinery of culture.

As it is, we've gotten the matter turned around in a typical collectivist, authoritarian approach. We should realize that people do not exist for the benefit of family and society. Family and society exists for the benefit of people. This is not to say that people should be selfish and live for themselves; it is to say that people have more value in the eyes of God than institutions. Jesus died for individuals, not for a local church, a state, a business, or even a family. Institutions can be reformed, but they cannot redeemed because they will the go way of all the earth.

Even in the Garden of Eden, God did not say, "It not good that there is no one available for marriage, so I'll create people for the institution." No it was the other way around: marriage, like the Sabbath, was created for man. Once family or society ceases to be of benefit to the individuals who constitute these institutions, we must ask if these institutions are acting legitimately or if they are corrupt. As a case in point, if modern marriage has nothing meaningful to offer to men today, we must ask if men should feel any more allegiance to the institution than the Reformers felt to the medieval Roman Catholic Church. Married men are required to honor their vows, but single men are not required to embrace a modern-day travesty of what God intended.

Granted, marriage is valuable for the experience of giving and receiving love when it functions properly. In fact, this is why I take umbrage with those commentators who rail against married people who have no children. Despite the zeal of many of these commentators, their position is unscriptural. Men and women are more than studs and brood-mares. We do not sire younglings for sake of those who rule over us. The Bible speaks of the one flesh relationship as a cause for marriage independent of childbearing (Gen. 2:18–25; 1 Cor. 7:2–6). Even when Jesus spoke of this relationship in Matthew 19, he mentioned nothing about the need to "be fruitful and multiply." If marriage has no worth apart from procreation and the rearing of children, then the marriages of infertile couples and the elderly are illegitimate and worthy of annulment. Who will defend such a proposition?

Marriage has worth whether it serves the economy or not, whether it serves the church or not, etc. In contrast, a utilitarian subordination of marriage to the interests of society leads us not only to debase, cheapen, and profane marriage, it also lead us down a path where we ironically devalue the very people we claim to cherish: poor people, old people, and children. Let us stop viewing human beings as pawns for the petty ambitions of those in power.

The Mysterious Calling

Debbie Maken, like many religious people, makes liberal use of the term "calling." On page 101, she remarks, "Marriage is what we're to pursue unless God specifically calls us to be single." Similar talk about being "called to marriage" or "called to singleness" abounds among many other believers. I, however, have yet to find one passage in the Bible that uses either of these catch phrases. In 1 Corinthians 7, for instance, it merely speaks of abiding in the state "*in* which" (not "*to* which") a person "is called" (v. 24). How does one get "called" to singleness or marriage as it is? Is there some mysterious revelation about matrimony given to the contemporary believer apart from what is already revealed in the Bible? Where are the Scriptures that talk about this type of revelation? Does one get "called to marriage" unless one is not attractive to the opposite sex? Does the "calling" happen about the time puberty commences, and does it wane when one skirts over the age of 35? Seriously, I think some people are confusing their own feelings and subjective experiences with a divine calling.

I suppose Mrs. Maken's book is an attempt to figure out God's "calling" for one's marital status without the need for mysterious revelations. It seems to boils down to the idea that unless your asexual, God expects you to get married. But as I have said repeatedly, her exegesis of the Scriptures doesn't support her case. Perhaps there are some who are going to come away frustrated from what I said, wondering how they will ever know if they should marry or not. I suppose Job was frustrated, too, since God never bothered to tell him why he was suffering. As it is, God never promised us a detailed road map for our lives to make the task of decision-making a cakewalk. I already warned against trying to peer through the heavens the way some peer into Magic 8-balls. Let us be content with the assurance God has given to his people about all things working together for their good (Rom. 8:28), and leave the secret things to him.

Those Who Just Can't Wait

Mrs. Maken concludes chapter 7 with the following thoughts:

"'Wait on the Lord'"

It's time for us to recognize that marriage is God's will for our lives and begin to pursue what God has in store for us. Passively waiting for what God has declared to be his will can only result in paying a price that is far too high ...

... In creating us for marriage, God had something truly divine in mind. When we see something ahead that God has told us is in store for us, let's act like kids on Christmas morning and run as fast as we can to get what he has prepared! (pp. 102–103)

I am a bit amused by this display of effervescent optimism. If we are to believe Mrs. Maken, marriage is everything great and a bag of chips on the side. I'll just note that as I write this, Mrs. Maken has not been married for a long time. I wonder what her attitude about marriage will be like seven years from now.

PART IX

Chapter 8
"'Jesus Is All You Need'"
(All You Need Is Love)

At the beginning of chapter 8 in *Getting Serious about Getting Married*, Debbie Maken discusses how others treated her when she was single. Consider her reaction to the people who questioned her about her love life: "'Seeing anyone special?' As a single woman, it seemed like parents, married friends, single friends, coworkers, and the rest of the world were bent on ferreting out every detail of any potential man in my life. Didn't people have anything else to ask me about—my job, my Bible study, the weather?" (p. 105). What I find so interesting about this opening statement is that Debbie Maken admits to being uncomfortable with the treatment she received. I say this, because now that Mrs. Maken is married, she seem more than eager to encourage the same kind of meddling in the affairs of single people that she chafed at in her younger years. Her proverbial ox isn't getting gored; it's someone else's reputation that can now be carved up. I just wonder if Mrs. Maken ever considered that the question, "Seeing anyone special?" is not as half as brash and prying as asking a man "what kind of eunuch" he is.

At any rate, Mrs. Maken goes on to discuss others who, when questioned about their singleness, seem to be much more positive and accepting of their condition than Mrs. Maken was when she had no husband. Mrs. Maken dismisses the claims of these people with skepticism. That many people can find peace and contentment in their singleness is apparently unfathomable to her.

Don't They Know It's the End of the World?

Perhaps many of my readers are too young to remember a Skeeter Davis tune called "The End of the World." It's an early sixties pop song, a paean to adolescent angst and unrequited love. Over pensive strings, the female vocalist laments, "Don't they know it's the end of the world/'Cause you don't love me any more?" It seems the same maudlin tone undergirds Mrs. Maken's narrative in chapter 8. From pages 107 to 108, Mrs. Maken details the sad and lonely lives of single women. We are lead to believe that their unhappiness underscores the futility many face in trying to find contentment in singleness. As sad and lonely as these women are, is their pain any more noteworthy than the pain others suffer in this life?

If Mrs. Maken thinks her tales of woe are a compelling case for her radical views on marriage, she is wasting her ink. True, single women are unhappy, but single men are unhappy, too. Married people are unhappy. Divorced people are unhappy. Widows and widowers are unhappy. Poor people are unhappy. Rich people are unhappy. The list goes on. If a man or woman wants to use Mrs. Maken's book as an excuse to be miserable, there is little I can do about that. However, I don't have to jump over the cliff with the others and fool myself into thinking a wedding is the magic bullet for any bleak outlook on life a person might have. I concede that women have a right to admit their loneliness and longing for a spouse, just as men do. They have a right to pursue marriage if they desire it, just as men do. What women don't have right to do is to assume that God expects most of humanity to be married or that men have an obligation to wed them.

Mrs. Maken says, "Women are waking up to find that feminist ideology has not satisfied their inner woman" (p. 108). Why didn't these women wake up when men and children were suffering as a result of feminism? How odd that it is only now that many women are changing their tune, muffling any brash talk about "independence" and analogies regarding fish and bicycles. Women have done a stellar job in demonizing and ostracizing men for over three decades. During this time, men's concerns have largely been deemed to be unimportant. It remains to be seen whether a significant number of women are now going to start paying attention to the concerns many men have, even as these same women are embracing a form of neo-traditionalism. In short, the talk of how happy or unhappy single women are represents just one piece of the larger puzzle that confronts us as a society. Their feelings are worth consideration, but not to exclusion of what men are experiencing.

All You Need Is Love

There is a prevailing sentiment in our society that everyone needs the physical and emotional intimacy that only a "significant other" can provide. Even among unbelievers, this notion is widely embraced. When is the last time you heard a man sing on the radio about how he doesn't need a woman?

Debbie Maken's book falls into the same mode of thinking. She says, "God did not design the vast majority of us to be content without a marriage partner. God designed the spouse-shaped void to be filled by a spouse" (p. 111). How does Mrs. Maken propose to fill the "spouse-shaped void" of those who don't win the popularity contest with the opposite sex? What about women with physical defects or men who don't have the mental capacity to provide for a family? What do we do with those who have been unscripturally divorced and cannot reconcile with their ex-spouses? They cannot remarry (Matt. 19:9; 1 Cor. 7:10–11), so what options do they have? Are all of the aforementioned people barred from cultivating the spiritual fruits of joy and peace in their lives because of their martial status (Gal. 5:22; Phil. 4:6–7)? Are they incapable of having the great gain that comes from godliness with contentment (1 Tim. 6:6)?

The Bible informs us that the commandments of God are not burdensome (1 John 5:3). Yet, I am left to infer from Mrs. Maken that single people cannot but find their existence to be a burden. Are we to assume that the dissatisfaction and sexual impurity of unmarried people underscores the uselessness of calling them to chastity and learning to rest in the Lord? In short, has God failed single people? I think not. In actuality, the "spouse-shaped void" of which Mrs. Maken speaks can be filled to a great extent without the benefit of a marriage. It can be filled when people realize that marriage is not necessarily a gateway to happiness or success. It can be filled when we reject the lies our popular culture tells us about needing physical intimacy. It can be filled when people start taking responsibility for their own contentment and peace, instead of foisting their responsibility on the opposite sex. When we start living proactively in this regard, the "spouse-shaped void" can look rather small after a while.

Name It and Claim It vs. Claim Her and Name Her

Mrs. Maken goes on to complain about the popular notion that spiritually mature people are always happy. This is especially a problem with the "health and wealth" gospel, which attributes poverty and sickness to a lack of faith. In Mrs. Maken's view, the same flawed attitude lies behind the idea that single people shouldn't be sad but should instead trust in God to meet their need for a spouse (p. 112). I am glad that Mrs. Maken takes aim at prosperity theology; however, I could easily imagine a religionist saying: "Are you sad that women don't pay attention to you? You must not be trusting God enough and are not fulfilling your biblical mandate to seek a wife!" Instead of categorizing this position as the "name it and claim it" approach of prosperity theology, we could use the phrase *claim her and name her* (as in a woman taking a man's last name). Mrs. Maken fails to realize that the marriage mandate theology to which she subscribes is actually a sibling of the "health and wealth gospel." One theology has the same naive optimism, overemphasis on earthly blessings, and false standards of piety as the other.

To Mrs. Maken's credit, her criticism of what I would term *emotional correctness* in religion is warranted. The idea that Christians must "grin and bear it" and deny any feelings of sadness, anger, frustration, fear, etc. is unscriptural and downright absurd. Anyone who believes that Christians must be joyful in all circumstances needs to read Ecclesiastes 3:4 (as Mrs. Maken notes), the Psalms, or even the account of our Savior's emotional anguish in the Garden of Gethsemane. Having said this, I note that single men have been attacked by the agents of emotional correctness like women have. When men voice their concerns about how they are treated by women and society, they are dismissed as bitter "whiners" who can't get anyone to date them.

Furthermore, why does Mrs. Maken advocate the *claim her and name her* approach for men but allow women to take what I would call the *blame him and shame him* approach? She says at the bottom of page 114, "Feeding our frustration towards men in protracted adolescence can result in the misguided belief that we're better off without them or that we as single women are somehow better than single men." What effect does she think her book will have in this regard? Is Mrs. Maken not the same woman who, in chapter 4, targeted single men and their supposed "lack of male leadership" as the "true cause of protracted singleness"? I find her book to be little more than an invitation for women to sink into despair and animosity towards men.

Seeking One's Desire and Seeking God

When considering the matter of contentment, it is best to look at life as a game (see 1 Corinthians 9:24–25). We should play by the rules of the Creator, do our best, and live with the outcome like a good contestant. In this fashion, we can avoid the extremes of complacency on one hand and bitterness on the other hand.

I think Mrs. Maken is right to challenge the notion that we must be resigned to live with whatever situation life throws at us. She speaks of the self-defeating approach some take to marriage in this regard: "Many of us have been taught that we must become completely neutral or numb to the idea of marriage before God will bless us with it" (p. 116). Clearly, this line of thinking is unprofitable, yet we must also note that our desires cannot dethrone our allegiance to our Creator. Again, there is a balance to be struck between complacency on one hand and bitterness on the other hand (or covetousness for that matter).

As far as pursuing marriage is concerned, Mrs. Maken is right to make a distinction between "self-interest" and "selfishness." As she says, "Self-interest is not selfishness. Self-interest only becomes unholy when we organize our lives apart from God" (Ibid.). Far be it from me to question the desire many people have for a spouse. I only wonder why Debbie Maken and those of her persuasion do not return the same courtesy to those will not marry and/or have children. Single people and childless couples are frequently belittled as being selfish. In fact, I suspect the charge of selfishness is often raised as *prima facie* evidence that single people and childless couples are living in sin. Will we judge others with the same measure by which we want ourselves to be judged (Matt. 7:2)?

Conclusion

At the end of chapter 8, Mrs. Maken raises the ugly specter of those who teach the "doctrine of demons" by forbidding others to marry (1 Tim. 4:15). She writes: "I anticipate that those who defend the status quo on singleness will retort that they did not forbid marriage but only told singles to not overelevate marriage in hopes that then they would be not be overly disappointed for not being married. In other words, be neutral. We cannot escape the fact that this new doctrine actually creates an artificial tension between the Maker and something that he declared to be good. They make marriage to appear to be in competition with the One who made it. It is not" (p. 117). Mrs. Maken is simply raising a straw man here. Teaching someone to prioritize their desires in life is a far cry from telling them to be neutral to what they would otherwise want. Teaching someone the value of contentment is not the same as embracing resignation. Mrs. Maken decries the "artificial tension" some supposedly place between God and marriage. I will simply say that our Lord himself suggested some tension in Luke 14:35: "If anyone comes after Me and does not hate his father and mother, wife and children, brothers and sisters, yes, and his own life also, he cannot be My disciple." We should not take Jesus' statement as a total rejection of marriage and family, but such things cannot be seen as necessary avenues of sanctification. They must be put in their proper place.

Mrs. Maken's mistake is rejecting one extreme for another. True, the fatalism that many singles have about their situation is not necessary. Jesus does not demand that we negate every single desire we have in life for things other than him. But we must desire his will even more than our own. We must not become bitter when life does not reward us with what we want. We must not assume that we are entitled to partake of the blissful fruits of matrimony. Many people are aware of the prayer that asks God to grant the wisdom to discern between those things one can and cannot change. Let us have the same attitude towards our marital status. Our desires for many things in this life are lawful, but in the end, Jesus is most assuredly "all we need."

PART X

Chapter 9
"'Being Single = Knowing and Serving God Better'"
(You Don't Know Like I Know)

I am certain many, if not most, of my readers are familiar with 1 Corinthians 7:32–34. In this passage we read that the unmarried "cares for the things of the Lord" whereas the married "cares about the things of the world," that is, pleasing a spouse. Some probably come away from this passage believing singleness is better than marriage if only for the benefit of offering service and devotion to God without distraction. Debbie Maken, however, takes issue with such a notion. In chapter 9 of her book, she alleges not only that married people can serve God in a comparable fashion to single people, but also that married people have an intimate understanding of God single people do not have.

Singles, Sherpas, and Selfishness

At the bottom of page 119, Mrs. Maken says she could never understand why others expected her to do more for ministry when she was single. She goes on to explain how married people can divide labor for daily tasks the way single people cannot. We should applaud Mrs. Maken for challenging the myth that single people always have more time for church activities than married people. I wonder why so many religious leaders act as if the personal time of single people is more expendable in this regard. Maybe the reason is because many think singles have a proclivity towards being selfish. I have previously discussed how the charge of selfishness is often hurled at single people, but I want to say a little more about this matter. Consider what one author recently wrote about single men:

> Are there not biblical indicators of whether one should seek marriage? Would you agree that immature men who employ their singleness for selfish indulgence (e.g., excessive golf or other hobbies, spending a high percentage of their salary on entertainment) would be well-served (with respect to their Christian sanctification) by having to bear the huge personal responsibility of a wife? Granted, they must have a modicum of maturity even to marry, but that minimum standard being met, marriage matures and sancti-

fies them (far beyond the accountability of male roommates, I might add). Many married men readily testify that their wife has been used of God as a great (even the greatest) instrument towards their sanctification. To lack this instrument would have been to stunt their sanctification, would it not?[1]

So are married people, by default, less selfish than single people? Or is the selfishness of one often simply traded for the selfishness of the group? Apparently, some are not familiar with the old saying about God blessing "us four and no more." This saying pretty much sums up the shallowness of what often passes for religious conservatism in this society. He who is without sin in this matter may cast the first stone at single people. A bachelor may indeed have his "golf or other hobbies" but married people have their weddings, receptions, honeymoons, McMansions, oversized SUVs, pontoon boats, family vacations, amusement parks, toys for the kids, and piano lessons for Junior to make the parents proud. As a lawful as these things are, I fail to see how they bring a soul any closer to God than the time a single man spends in front of the computer playing NetHack.

In fact, if marriage is a cure for selfishness, then why do we hear of rampant divorce, adultery, domestic violence, and all the other social ills that seem plague only those who insist on finding a mate? As it is, singles may have extra time to pursue their individual interests, but married people have the privilege of enjoying physical and emotional intimacy with a given spouse. Life is full of trade-offs, so why do we begrudge others the fruit for which we were not willing to pay the price? When a married person criticizes a single person's use of time, such criticism may be an indication of an envious heart. Some commentators simply need to consider their motivations for being so censorious towards the unmarried.

The bottom line is marriage is neither a necessary nor reliable cure for selfishness. So many married people who claim to have less time for the Lord than single people seem to have plenty of time to do all the unnecessary things they want to do, including enjoying many things a single person cannot enjoy. Let's look again at what 1 Cor.7:32–34 says. It does not say a married person has less time for church activities than a single person. It says a married person's interests are divided between the Lord and a spouse. Think about that.

What application can we make from what I've said? Simply this: Religious leaders have no business treating single people like a band of Sherpas to take up the loads that married people ought to bear. Too many married pundits who talk of single people "having more time" sound a lot like the man in Luke 14:20: "I have married a wife, and therefore cannot come." The fact of matter is that *all our time* belongs to the Lord, including the time we spend on recreational pursuits not only as single people, but as families as well. Just because a single man has more time for individual interests than a married man does not mean we can engage in arrogant surmisings about what the single man is doing or should be doing with his free moments. Such judgments are between a single person and the Lord (Rom. 14:1–13).

The Church - Family of God or Just Godly Families?

Continuing on in chapter 9 of Debbie Maken's book, we read that families play a necessary part in the expansion of God's kingdom. Mrs. Maken writes:

> God's plan for kingdom expansion has always involved marriage and family. Even the New Testament gives priority to the nuclear family when it comes to increasing the kingdom: "For the promise is for you and for your children and for all who are far off, everyone whom the Lord our Gods calls to himself" (Acts 2:39). The early church grew as families were saved "household to household."
>
> This expansion always starts at home and works itself outward ("in Jerusalem and in all Judea and Samaria, and to the end of the earth," Acts 1:8), not the other way around. (pp. 121–122)

With all due respect to Mrs. Maken, she is simply misapplying the Scripture in a rather egregious manner. That people were saved "household to household" no more implies the need for families in God's plan of redemption than God's call to the poor (James 2:5) implies that we must embrace poverty in order to be saved. Family or no family, every soul must come to Christ individually. The faith of a given family cannot sanctify or save a person (Ezek. 18:1–23).

Sure, family units do have something to contribute to a local church, and some do indeed learn the gospel from their parents. There is, however, no guarantee that this always holds true. Family religion can sometimes be a stumbling-block to one's acceptance of biblical truths (Matt. 10:34–36). Let us also note that Mrs. Maken cannot defend her statement about the expansion of the Church always starting "at home." The passage she quotes (Acts 1:8) has nothing to do with families; it simply draws attention to the fact that salvation came to the Jews first and then to the Gentiles (Rom. 1:16).

You Don't Know Like I Know

As if Mrs. Maken's understanding of the scheme of redemption wasn't flawed enough, the rest of chapter 9 only gets worse. Mrs. Maken says on page 124: "God has purposely made himself known through familial relationships. Such relationships—husband, wife, daughter, son—show us part of the divine nature of God. When we fail to marry, whether through our own fault or cultural fault, we miss out on this means that God has established to know him more deeply and intimately." Really? Has marriage mandate theology finally come to this? Are we to embrace a wacky form of Gnosticism where the deeper mysteries of the Godhead come through an initiation into the Cult of the Married Ones? I thought a Christian received "all things that pertained to life and godliness" through knowledge of Christ (2 Peter 1:2–3) and that such knowledge came by hearing and obeying the Word of God (John 20:30–31; 2 Tim. 3:14–17; Rom. 10:17; 1 John 2:3–5). Perhaps we should cover ourselves with duct tape, roll around in a pile of sheared wool, get on all fours, and start chewing cud so that we may know how Jesus cares for us the way a shepherd cares for sheep. Seriously, do we appreciate the difference between metaphorical and literal language, or the difference between types and antitypes? What vital knowledge does marriage give me about the Trinity that I cannot already glean from the Scriptures?

Have we forgotten what Ephesians 5:25 says? Paul did not write, "Husbands, know that God loves you the way you love your wives." The Apostle already took for granted that his male audience knew how Jesus loved the Church. In case they didn't know, they were given the essentials in verses 26–27. What wasn't so certain was if the Ephesian men knew how to love their wives. In other words, the Ephesians seemed to have already grasped the relationship between Christ and Church before knowing what marriage was intended to be. Here is clear proof that marriage does not impart the special knowledge of divine realities that some people think it does.

In essence, chapter 9 is yet another section rife with implausible statements. I concede we cannot be so presumptuous to think that single Christians are, by default, more devoted to God than married people. Those who take Debbie Maken's position on marriage are justifiably opposed to such thinking. However, claiming that married people have a special knowledge of God that single people do not have is utterly preposterous. Mrs. Maken simply ought to know better than proffer such a claim, but considering what I have covered thus far, I am not surprised she goes to such extremes in her writing.

PART XI

Chapter 10
"'Single = Celibate'"
(The Sex Mandate?)

Imagine a preacher standing up before his congregation on Sunday morning and declaring, "Single people, God commands you to get married and to have sex!" I am certain there are plenty of singles in their late teens and early twenties that would secretly delight for this pronouncement to be made. A young man, with his hormones raging and his frontal lobe not fully developed, could declare, "I have no choice but to fulfill God's mandate and pursue that really good-looking sister in Christ I met in Bible camp last Summer. We'll get married and our ticket to paradise will be punched!" You may think I jest, but in chapter 10 of *Getting Serious about Getting Married*, Debbie Maken defends the notion that we are "hardwired by our Creator to want sex and to pursue sexual fulfillment" (p. 128).

Are we really "hardwired" to want and pursue sex? Forgive me for turning on the cold shower, but the idea that we have no choice but to have sex and therefore we should marry is a naive and harmful myth. It is not taught by the Scriptures. I am certain a few jaws will drop at this statement; therefore, permit me to explain why I have come to the conclusions that I have.

Design and "God-Given" Desires

When religious leaders talk about human sexuality and God's design, they often assert that marriage is the proper avenue for the expression of our "God-given desires." The truth, however, is that our desire for sex is *not* "God-given." How can this be? Simple. We must distinguish between sexual response (which is biological), and desire (which is an act of the will). We make a similar distinction when we consider food. For instance, a woman may notice that someone has brought some store-bought turtle cheesecake to her workplace. The woman's mouth may salivate, but if she is on a diet, she may lose her desire after reading the nutrition label or list of ingredients on the side of the packaging. In this case, we see the desire for food, which is even stronger and more necessary than the desire for sex, can be extinguished by choice.

We need food to survive and sooner or later, we must desire and eat food. The same cannot be said about sex. Paul corrected the Corinthians when he declared:

> All things are lawful for me, but all things are not helpful. All things are lawful for me, but *I will not be brought under the power of any*. Foods for the stomach and the stomach for foods, but God will destroy both it and them. Now the body is not for sexual immorality but for the Lord, and the Lord for the body. (1 Cor. 6:12–13) (emphasis mine)

If there was ever a time for Paul to concede that our reproductive organs had to be used for sex the way our stomach must be used for food, this verse would probably be the place. Paul, however, makes no such concession. He simply tells the Corinthians that the body is "not for sexual immorality." Sexual activity is not an inevitability. Indeed, when we declare that God indiscriminately gives people a desire for sex, then we call into question what the Bible plainly declares about his nature:

> Let no one say when he is tempted, "I am tempted by God"; for God cannot be tempted by evil, *nor does He Himself tempt anyone*. But each one is tempted when he is drawn away by *his own desires* and enticed. (James 1:13–15) (emphasis mine)

> No temptation has overtaken you except such as is common to man; but God is faithful, who *will not allow you to be tempted beyond what you are able*, but with the temptation will also *make the way of escape, that you may be able to bear it*. (1 Cor. 10:13) (emphasis mine)

Remember, that sexual arousal like hunger does not wait on a time table. Your body does not know whether your are married or not. When it responds to stimuli, it is prepared for an act that might as well take place immediately. If we confuse innate sexual responses with "God-given desires," then we are claiming that God hasn't really programmed us to want sex in marriage, per se, as much as he has programmed us to want sex *right away*.

Debbie Maken says, "There must be hope of a timely marriage for abstinence to be successful" (p. 132). This hope, however, is often dashed by unrealistic demands placed on both sexes (especially demands placed on men). We must also acknowledge that there will be some people who cannot get married under any reasonable circumstances. So how can we say to a single man that he is programmed to want and pursue sex when there is *no immediate prospect of him getting married*? What "way of escape" does he have from his desires in that case? Sexual activity outside of marriage would most certainly be a problem for him. I cannot but wonder how many Christians have succumbed to this defeatist thinking. Christians might say, "God made me this way. I am so lonely. I have needs and they have to be met." Consequently, they might give themselves permission to get angry at God, use pornography, sleep around, get unscripturally remarried, or commit adultery.

I anticipate someone will point to 2 Thessalonians 3:10 and claim that just as men have to work in order to eat, so they must work to obtain the favor of godly women in pursuit of marriage. This line of reasoning fails under closer scrutiny, however. We give food to who are starving, disabled, or unable to work, but we don't grant sex to those *who will never have a chance to marry through no fault of their own*. Is God a respecter of persons that we should supply benevolence for one perceived human need but not for another? The restrictions God places on sexuality are much more stringent than what he places on other biological drives. Moreover, as a man, I realize that finding some sort of employment to secure the basic necessities of life is not as difficult as finding the kind of employment needed to satisfy the demands of many a religious woman in this consumeristic society. We don't tell a male teenager that he has to wait to get out on his own before he can eat, but we say that he must do so if he wants to get married. We don't tell a young man that he has no choice but to buy all of his food from the most expensive grocery store in town, but we declare he has no choice but to embrace the expensive proposition of marriage in order to gratify his sexual desires. If you balk at the idea of equating sex with a cheap commodity like food, then you should not talk about men having to labor as if such were the case.

In short, the desire for sex is not like the desire for food, drink, sleep, etc. When we tell single people that God programmed them to seek out sex, then we set them up for failure. This is why the Marriage Mandate Movement is not a harmless fad. We must stand up and combat any false doctrine that causes Christians to yield to temptation in a fit of helplessness or causes them to question God's justice and love.

Is Marriage the Cure for Being Hot and Bothered?

Debbie Maken claims in chapter 10 that our sex drive "was designed to find release in marriage" (p. 128). She then references 1 Corinthians 7:1–2 as a proof-text for encouraging single people to get married. I have already indicated in part 3 of my review that an application of 1 Corinthians 7:1–2 to single people is a violation of the context. Paul was addressing married Christians in that passage.

When I recently pointed out the context of 1 Corinthians 7:1–2 to some people, one critic wanted to know why Paul would demand married people have sexual relations to address the problem of self-control, but not demand something similar for single people. After all, doesn't sexual temptation affect single people to a greater extent than married people? In answer to this question, let me point out that the being married to someone and yet being forced to go without sex is more frustrating than not being married at all. We kid ourselves if we believe someone who is accustomed to having a physical relationship with another person can continue to live in close quarters with the other person and yet have no problem when the intimacy suddenly stops. In response to this observation, my critic declared my viewpoint to be a "bald assertion." I suppose if we follow my critic's line of reasoning, boyfriends and girlfriends who live together are no more susceptible to sexual tension and temptation than those who live apart. Do we really believe that?

At any rate, Mrs. Maken continues her misapplication of 1 Corinthians 7:1–2 by pointing to Jesus' teaching in Matthew 5:28: "But I say to you that everyone who looks at a woman with lustful intent has already committed adultery with her in his heart" (ESV). Mrs. Maken suggests that since a lot of Christians are already guilty of sexual impurity according to Jesus, they need to get married to "avoid fornication," as per Paul's instructions.

Quite frankly, the idea that marriage can prevent people from having impure thoughts about others is downright laughable. There is no strong guarantee that marriage can keep you from falling into sexual sin. If such were the case, then adultery, online affairs, and married men looking at pornography would not be widespread problems. A well-known book among Evangelicals, *Every Man's Battle*, has this to say about marriage stemming lust:

> That marriage doesn't eliminate sexual impurity comes as no surprise to married men, although it does for teens and young singles ... Young singles believe that marriage creates a state of sexual nirvana ...
>
> But freedom from sexual sin rarely comes through marriage or the passage of time. (The phrase "dirty old man" should tell us something about that.) So if you're tired of sexual impurity and of the mediocre, distant relationship with God that results from it, quit waiting for marriage or some hormone drop to save the day.[1]

Here we have the unglamorous truth about sexuality in marriage. As a man, I cannot depend on any woman to keep me pure. I must do that myself.

With respect to 1 Corinthians 7:1–7, we might presume that conjugal duties might offer some insurance against sexual frustration in marriage, but even here there is no guarantee. Apart from the differences between men and women in how sex is viewed, there are the stressors of life to consider such as caring for children, illness, and separation. If a man thinks he can clobber a less than willing spouse into having sex with him by using 1 Corinthians 7:1–7, he will find himself disappointed by the half-hearted compliance given to him. Do you know what it is like to embrace someone who is frigid towards you?

Nice Ladies Who Don't (At All)

Debbie Maken says in her book: "Let me be totally honest with you. Though I got married at age thirty-one, I really could have used a husband at sixteen, seventeen, nineteen, twenty-one, twenty-three, twenty-seven, twenty-nine, thirty. Especially at twenty-five—a year of numerous cold showers. Let's be honest, being single doesn't make you not want sex. Whoever said that age thirty-four is a woman's sexual peak needs to be shot" (p. 127). I find this confession to be mildly humorous. Quite frankly, as a man, I could have used a wife at age twelve or thirteen if we want to look at the matter that way. Where were the Christian women with Debbie Maken's level of desire when I was in my twenties? I suppose that today's Christian woman is more in touch with her sexuality than women of the past, and yet I wonder if Mrs. Maken is an exception to the rule just the same.

There are still probably women who see sex only in terms of having children or something to be bartered for a husband's good behavior. They may otherwise regard the act to be a major inconvenience. Just how understanding can men expect women to be about male sexuality? Consider this quote from *Every Man's Battle* regarding how women react to the sexual struggles men face: "Remember, our habits are rooted in our maleness. *We* understand them. Women don't. Almost without fail, women who hear about your sexual impurity will think of you as a pervert ... I know some men will disagree with me on this point, and that's fine, because you know your own wife better than I do. But most wives react with shock and revulsion rather than mercy and prayer."[2] Perhaps the authors of the book are basing their observations on what they've experienced with their female contemporaries. Maybe younger religious women have a more sympathetic and long-suffering understanding about male sexuality. Who is to say? Whatever the case, I daresay many young religious men have allowed popular culture to mislead them about what they can expect from women. Most religious women probably do not have the time, inclination, knowledge or stamina to play the part of the full-time seductress for their husbands.

In fact, Christian men have done a disservice to themselves by the swallowing the lie that pretty woman hold the key to sexual nirvana. Commercials, risqué movies, and pornography deceives us with the myth of the Sex Goddess. She doesn't exist, or if she does, she'll never sleep with you. Men need to be more discerning with regard to women they find physically attractive. Such women probably have had more than their share of attention from suitors. What incentive do women have to develop a personality or make themselves appealing in other ways when men lavish attention on them so freely? Is it any wonder that many physically attractive women turn out be utterly ignorant, narcissistic, or both? Do we expect such self-centered creatures to pause a moment and consider to how best satisfy the physical and emotional desires of the men in their lives?

On top of this, consider that our culture in its misguided spirit of chivalry has given deference to female sexuality at the expense of male sexuality. Female sexuality seen as a complex, mysterious thing demanding the unqualified reverence of men. Male sexuality is regarded with exasperated disdain or regarded as a simplistic matter that requires little, if any, attention. Is it any wonder that many men end up sexually frustrated in marriage because their desires are counted as a trivial matter? As Mr. Spock would say, "After a time, you may find that having is not so pleasing a thing, after all, as wanting."

Is That All There Is?

I think religious leaders and popular culture have much in common by being guilty of sensationalizing the "first time." Young Christians may foolishly believe their honeymoon will usher in a state of inexplicable marital bliss. In actuality, their first experience with the conjugal act may be a very awkward and disappointing affair. Sex is more than hot bodies and technique. The amount of satisfaction married people get from sex depends upon mutual understanding and respect between the husband and wife. Such mutual understanding and respect takes time and effort. Hence, satisfying sex is the blossom, not the taproot of a good marriage. This is why I take umbrage with the cheery attitude of many Evangelical writers who sell some rosy picture of sex in marriage. The humdrum of marriage life is a reality. Habituation and boredom is an ever present threat. Marriage takes hard work. Mrs. Maken's sexually frustrated readers probably haven't thought through these matters, though.

In essence, it is dangerous to base our relationships with the opposite sex on physical attraction. Even in a good marriage, satisfying sex is not always a guarantee. Being trapped in a loveless marriage can be just as destructive in its earthly consequences as having sex outside of marriage. Sex is never safe, even when sanctioned by the church.

When Single People Fail

Debbie Maken writes that adolescents will not wait to get married before having sex if they see older singles caught in indefinite singleness without a clear hope for marriage (p. 130). Thus, Mrs. Maken's general premise in chapter 10 is that Christian singles need to hurry up and get married for the sake of sexual purity. I note Mrs. Maken's line of argumentation is inconsistent with something she says later: "We cannot point to the high divorce rate and say that it's better not to marry. That's like saying you shouldn't go to high school because the dropout rate is increasing. The failure of other people's marriage is no reason to scrap marriage altogether" (p. 138). Let's be consistent. If we can't point to other people's failures as an excuse not to marry, then we can't point to other people's failures as an excuse to rush into marriage, either. I admit that premarital sex and the divorce rate are *both* problems. Mrs. Maken's radical pro-marriage agenda doesn't really get to heart of either of these issues, though.

Why do so many religious singles have a difficult time staying pure? The main reason is they have internalized the false notion that human beings are programmed to have sex. This like saying that human beings are programmed to play soccer. We may be biologically equipped to perform both acts, but we have a choice about having sex, just as we do about kicking a ball. I have already refuted the idea that our desires are "God-given." We are human beings, not fish making a salmon run.

It is a mistake to believe that we will necessarily cause ourselves physical or psychological harm if we refrain from sex. Some experts may point to some ways in which sex benefits our bodies, but in terms of physical well-being, I believe good nutrition, adequate rest, and exercise can easily make up for any loss that comes from celibacy. As for psychological well-being, celibacy does not intrinsically pose a threat in that case either. Even Abraham Maslow, the humanist psychologist who formulated the "hierarchy of needs," conceded as much:

> An ever-recurring question is: Does sexual deprivation inevitably give rise to all or any of the many effects of frustration, e.g., aggression, sublimation, etc. It is now well known that many cases are found in which celibacy has no psychopathological effects. In many other cases, however, it has many bad effects. What factor determines which shall be the result? Clinical work with non-neurotic people gives the clear answer that sexual deprivation becomes pathogenic in a severe sense only when it is felt by the individual to represent rejection by the opposite sex, inferiority, lack of worth, lack of respect, or isolation. Sexual deprivation can be borne with relative ease by individuals for whom it has no such implications. (Of course, there will probably be what Rosenzweig calls need-persistive reactions, but these are not necessarily pathological.)[3]

While some may not believe that celibacy will cause harm, they still maintain that sex is a transcending event that no average human being should go without. Our popular culture considers the lives of those who don't have sex as being sad and pitiful. However, we don't talk about emotionally empty souls who hop from one bed to another in a string of failed relationships. We don't talk about the sexually addicted who become numb as they fall into a downward spiral of trying to seek out more intense experiences and new highs. We don't talk about people stuck in loveless marriages who have sex in a perfunctory manner, but are intensely unhappy. As Eleanor Daniel writes: "What a single person perceives as sexual needs may, in fact, be desires for companionship, emotional security, closeness, affirmation, love. Very often, a person's specific physical needs are significantly reduced when the other needs are met."[4] Of course, I would add that sex is not a "need" at all.

Besides inaccurate beliefs about our biological programming, the second main reason many single people fail to stay pure is that it's hard to resist something if you have *already made up your mind that you want it*. Again, what does the Bible say we are led away by when we are tempted? Our "own desires." John Piper puts it another way: "It's a burden to be sexually chaste if you believe the message of the world that fornication or adultery really will give you more satisfaction."[5] If you look at something as forbidden fruit, you are still looking at it as fruit, period. Some fruits, however, are downright poisonous. Many people need to change their desires if they want to stop struggling with staying sexually pure. We need to do some soul-searching and ask ourselves some pointed questions. Why do we want things that we know we are not allowed to have? What do we expect to get by receiving what we desire? Are our expectations realistic? Have we weighed the costs and benefits? Have we considered what receiving what we desire will do to ourselves, to others, and to our relationship with God? I suspect that many Christians do not go through this type of examination, so they leave themselves unprepared when temptation hits them. In short, a major cure for sexual temptation is deciding that you *don't want sex*!!

Self-Control and Celibacy

On page 128 of Debbie Maken's book, she tells her readers: "Celibacy and abstinence are not the same. Celibacy and singleness are not the same. Celibacy and self-control are not the same. Celibacy is a gift of God in which he has removed the drive to pursue sex." In contrast to Mrs. Maken, however, the *American Heritage Dictionary* provides us with a different definition of celibacy: "*abstention* from sexual intercourse, especially by reason of religious vows" or the "condition of being unmarried."[6] I daresay our English dictionaries are probably a better guide than Mrs. Maken on understanding what celibacy is. Remember that in Matthew 19, Jesus said some "made themselves eunuchs." Clearly, celibacy is a matter where one exercises free will. Mrs. Maken seems to confuse celibacy with *asexuality*, but these two "are not the same."

You may express disbelief at my claim about celibacy and free-will. You may think that very few people have the ability to remain single and chaste indefinitely. Indeed, many people talk about self-control being a gift. Self-control, however, is not a gift. It is a commandment in the Bible. Indeed, some readers may not realize that the terms "sober" and "temperate" in our English Bibles are merely translations of the Greek word for self-control (1 Cor. 9:25; Gal. 5:23; 2 Peter 1:6).

If They Cannot Contain

What are we to make, then, of 1 Corinthians 7:8–9? Here the Apostle Paul says, "But to the unmarried and to the widows: It is good for them if they remain even as I am; but if they cannot exercise self-control, let them marry. For it is better to marry than to burn with passion." Shall we assume from this verse that the Apostle is admonishing sexually frustrated singles to get married (as Debbie Maken asserts in chapter 10)? I have examined this passage in part 3 of my critique, and as I noted, this is verse is not addressing the sexual desires of unmarried people, per se, as much as it is addressing those ensnared in illicit relationships. First of all, let us remember that the phrase "cannot contain" is a bad translation; the verse should be rendered "if they *will not* exercise self-control." Also, we should note that to "burn in passion" is an act that the Apostle Paul casts in a bad light. It cannot be defined as sexual arousal, per se, for the simple fact that married people, like single people, experience this sensation. If we define the phrase "to burn" in 1 Corinthians 7:8–9 as sexual arousal, then we are put in the awkward position of demanding that married people be asexual (it would be "better to be married than to have sexual desire")! Yet, the Bible commends sexual arousal for married people (Prov. 5:18–19). The phrase "to burn" must, of necessity, refer to some sinful sexual behavior.

Paul is basically putting forth a conditional commandment in a less than ideal circumstance. This is not something unique for Paul; we see the same sort of reasoning employed in 1 Corinthians 7:10–11. In v. 10, the ideal circumstance is that people are not to divorce their spouses, but if they do, they are to remain unmarried (v. 11). Likewise, in 1 Corinthians 7:8–9, the ideal circumstance is that single Christians will practice self-control (as commanded by the Bible), but if they yield to their lusts, then it is better that they get married instead of continuing in sexual immorality. One individual has mistakenly assumed from my interpretation that I am condoning fornication before one can get married. This is absolute nonsense which arises from the foolish belief that sex is an inevitability. I am not suggesting that one first fall into temptation before considering marriage, nor am I suggesting that Christians seek to avoid marriage at all costs. What I am simply suggesting is that sexual frustration need not be a major reason for getting married (and it shouldn't be).

Celibacy Is Doable

Abstention from illicit sexual activity for an indefinite period of time is doable. Otherwise, the Bible is lying to us. The Apostle John tells us that God's commandments are not burdensome (1 John 5:3). This must, of necessity, include the commandment to be chaste. Those who have no hope of marriage have the promise of 1 John 5:3 or else Christianity doesn't apply to them.

Someone asked me how I account for single Christians who struggle with masturbation. What of it? Christians struggling with masturbation is proof of nothing except that Christians struggle with masturbation. If masturbation is a sin, then single Christians must have the assurance that they can resist it indefinitely without too much effort. If refraining from masturbation is an inherently difficult act that only a few can undertake, then the theology of some religious leaders who forbid masturbation is a sham. We must be consistent, regardless of what our convictions are about this issue.

At any rate, there are some sensible steps a single person can take to avoid sexual arousal and thus the uncomfortable tension that results from such arousal. The authors of *Every Man's Battle* suggest, among other tactics, that men "bounce" their eyes away from looking at attractive women. They also have the following to say about masturbation, which is worth some consideration: "Masturbation is a symptom of uncontrolled eyes and free-racing thoughts. When you create the new habits of bouncing your eyes and taking your thoughts captive, masturbation will cease. Until then, it won't. There's no sense in targeting masturbation itself, because you won't be attacking the real source of the problem. Target the eyes and mind instead."[7] In addition to "bouncing" the eyes, another line of defense is to think realistically about those that we are tempted to lust after. It is all too easy to drift into a fantasy about people that we don't really know. However, when we realize that person we desire is married, has emotional problems, is selfish, or has some other quality that makes a relationship with them an odious proposition, then we are not inclined to pursue them any further.

Regardless of whatever tactics we use to keep ourselves chaste, we must keep in mind that God's commandments are not inherently difficult. God does not set out to doom us to failure. We cause ourselves to fail when we yield to self-deception. The choice is ultimately ours.

Church-Sanctioned Sex - The Flip-Flopping of the Preachers

Religious leaders are oftentimes abysmally inconsistent about sexuality. Somehow many think they can use sexuality as a both a carrot and stick to get people married. All the same, there is no middle ground in the matter of self-control. If we are not predestined to lust or commit fornication, then we are not predestined to marry either.

If sexual desire is biblical proof for the need to get married, then we should demand that boys and girls marry the moment they reach puberty. Yet we don't do this. Somehow we assume that teenaged Christians can stay pure into their mid-twenties but are unable to do so well into their thirties, forties, or fifties. This line of thinking is absurd. Our bodies do not know anything about the socially acceptable time that religious pundits want us to get married. Sexual tension builds up in a matter of days or months, not years. If biology is destiny as Mrs. Maken and others seems to suggest, then teenagers are predestined to have sex sooner, not later.

Yet, as we have noted, the real reason that so many singles fail to be chaste is not because of biology, but because of discouragement, self-deception, or selfishness. Let's face it: The sex drive of older singles does not increase; it tapers off. Hence, the suggestion that older singles have an insurmountable problem controlling themselves to the degree we expect of younger singles is nothing short of hilarious. We can't have it both ways. We can't hold up a copy of *Every Young Man's Battle* and preach "self-control" to teenaged boys, but then turn around, hold up Mrs. Maken's book, and preach about "God-given desires" to thirty-something men. If we say an average man can be chaste in his sexual prime, then logic dictates that he can be chaste for the rest of his life.

There is something else that I find noteworthy about the current emphasis many Evangelicals place on marriage these days. It is that Evangelicals must confront the legacy of their own faith communities about sex. Perhaps preachers have done such an effective job of making young religious people afraid of sex that churches are now paying the price for their "success." For better or for worse, hostile and ambivalent messages about sexuality from our religious leaders are only going to make relationships between the sexes more difficult, not less. Granted, sexual purity is important, but one cannot be anti-sex and pro-marriage at the same time. Marriage and sexual desire stand or fall together.

If we go overboard in maintaining the purity of young people to the extent that we fail to present a positive, balanced, biblical view of sexuality, then we should be prepared to reap the consequences. There have been studies that indicate a correlation between judgmental attitudes towards sexuality and sexual dysfunction. Healthy marriages won't happen in this regard. As it is, I wonder if Mrs. Maken and her allies would really be so upbeat about marriage and sexuality if some conservative pundits weren't so anxious about declining church membership and shifting demographics in our culture.

Furthermore, what shall we do with those single Christians who, because of their ambivalence towards sexuality, find relationships with the opposite sex to be an uncomfortable matter? Shall we belittle them and tell them to just get over the emotional programming that may very well have been the result of their religious upbringing? In our attempt to get these people married, would our disregard for their conscientious scruples be a disregard for the convictions of "weaker" Christians, thus a violation of Romans 14? We need to ask ourselves these questions before corralling single Christians into the institution of marriage.

What Attitude Then?

One may wonder what my own attitude about sex is. I think that while it is an intrinsically positive aspect of God's creation, it is nonetheless overrated. Most of society's obsession with sex probably comes from an unprecedented openness about the subject matter and an unprecedented degree of interaction between men and women in public spaces. Society's obsession with sex is also probably the reason we have so much sin and sorrow in this world. This obsession has lead to the kind of status-seeking behaviors we see in our world today where women base their worth on physical beauty and men base their worth on having a woman. It also probably contributes to bigotry against single people. Just the same, sex only represents one facet of the human experience at best. At worst, it can be destructive, ruining the lives of the unmarried and married alike.

I have no antipathy towards sex, but neither does my happiness depend on it. The notion that men "only think of one thing" is a notion that I personally find insulting as a man. Many seem to think that men will tolerate various forms of mistreatment as long as they are thrown some meager scraps of physical intimacy on the side. I reject this dehumanizing viewpoint. I also reject the naive optimism of those who seek ineffable sexual bliss either beyond or within the confines of the marriage bed. Eleanor Daniel says it best: "When a person comes to grips with his sexuality, he is no longer dependent upon his marital status, or lack of it, to give him feelings of worth. He can go right on living with purpose and excitement, regardless of the stereotypes others may hold. He is well aware that he is neither biologically abnormal not totally unattractive if he isn't married. He need not be frustrated sexually—he simply finds creative, moral channels by which to express his sexuality. Self-acceptance is the key."[8]

Consider the alternatives. You can heed the message of Debbie Maken, other religionists, and the rest of popular culture and hang your head in shame because you are single. You can allow the devil to discourage you and make you feel less than human because you are not having sex. You can get angry at God when no one accepts you as a mate. You can be a slave to fashion and to the shallow tastes of ignorant and immature souls found among the opposite sex. You can sink into a mire of desperation, enter into ill-advised relationships, and ruin your happiness and peace of mind. You can be married to someone that you should have never married and be trapped in a prison much worse than the prison of loneliness.

I used to balk at the notion of going without sex for the rest of my life. Then I realized how my discontentment was only leaving me vulnerable to bitterness, depression, humiliation at the hands of others, temptation, and sexual sin. One has to learn self-control or end up being controlled by others. Also, a person should realize that the best reason for staying pure is not because one expects to get married, but because one desires to please God.

In short, you can unplug from the ungodly status quo. You can have your sexuality serve you instead of you serving your sexuality. You need not put yourself in a situation where you feel obligated to form an intimate relationship with someone. You can be open to the possibility of marriage; however, you can also defend your principles and say no to the opposite sex, if need be. Again, the choice is yours.

I like to finally address something Debbie Maken says in chapter 10 of her book: "God did not design us to be third wheels to married couples or buddies for other singles" (p. 133). If this statement is true, then I wonder why God even bothered to create the Church. We could all just practice family religion instead. I obviously think Mrs. Maken is incorrect in her assumptions. In our attempt to extol earthly families, let us not denigrate God's family. Marriages, and indeed sexuality, will cease one day, but the kingdom of the Lord will stand forever.

PART XII

Chapter 11
"A Few More 'Easy' Answers"
(Including a Few from Mrs. Maken)

In chapter 11 of *Getting Serious about Getting Married*, Debbie Maken focuses on a series of statements that she derisively terms "'easy' answers." Supposedly, these are "answers" often used to dismiss the concerns that single Christians raise about pursuing marriage. What follows is my own commentary, given partially in response to Mrs. Maken's reply to the "'easy' answers":

1. "You have to be the right person to meet the right person."

Mrs. Maken is correct in taking this mantra to task. While a modicum of maturity is necessary for marriage, human beings are not perfect (not even for each other). Our world is full of mediocre people who have somehow managed to find loyal mates while more mature people go without spouses. And as far as being the "right person" is concerned, I think self-improvement is best undertaken for its own value and not for pleasing a member of the opposite sex.

2. "It's better to be single than to wish you were." ("Marriage is hard.")

I agree with this statement. Mrs. Maken, on the other hand, has an interesting response: "Life is hard. So is work, so is having a baby, so is parenting, so is being alone. Their are trade-offs in every station of life—challenges and benefits" (p. 138). Indeed. I therefore wonder why Mrs. Maken and others portray marriage in so lofty a manner as if no other mode of existence can bring one happiness.

Mrs. Maken goes on to mention that people should look to happily married Christian couples as a form of encouragement. She also avers, "We cannot pretend that a good marriage is a random, luck-of-the-draw event, and so it's better to avoid marriage as a solution" (Ibid.). Yet we cannot deny that there are a lot of people who are unhappily married as well. Granted, Mrs. Maken is correct in saying that a good marriage is not an accident, but there are many good people who still have difficult marriages for all their effort and best intentions. People cannot predict the changes that will occur in fortune, their mates, or themselves. It is utterly foolish to think that marriage is game of fixed rules wherein one can "beat the odds" by sheer skill (Eccl. 9:11). Making wise decisions can reduce some risks, but not all of them.

3. *"As soon as you stop looking, you'll find the right person."*

To some extent, I can see why Mrs. Maken takes issue with this statement. Passivity is not going to get one closer to matrimony. However, I do believe that spending too much time looking for a spouse is not a good idea, either. One should never act out of desperation. For one thing, desperation tends to drive away the very people we want to attract. Secondly, acting out of desperation causes one to make foolish and rash decisions. If the idea of being single for the rest of your life frightens you, then you are making yourself vulnerable to problems down the road through your own fears and passions.

There is no need to waste time casting a net if the fish are not biting. If there are no good prospects for marriage, then one should concentrate on self-improvement in spiritual and temporal matters. Fretting and obsessing over one's singleness is a useless waste of energy. Just as worry cannot change one's hair from white to black, worrying cannot change one's marital status. The command to "seek ye first the kingdom of God" is applicable today as it was thousands of years ago (Matt. 6:33).

4. *"You'll get married in God's perfect time so just relax!"*

Like Mrs. Maken, I disagree with this idea, but for a different reason. Mrs. Maken's objection focuses on the need for Christians to be proactive in their lives and not wait for God's "perfect time." My objection is that it is presumptuous to assume God has a spouse for us in his "perfect time" or otherwise. Everything I have written thus far bears witness to the fact that none of us are entitled to marriage anymore than we are entitled to $100,000. In fact, many marriages will cost at least that much.

5. *"My sister got married the other day, and she's thirty-seven."*

In response to those who optimistically point to the prospect of later marriages, Mrs. Maken brings up the case of one woman and remarks: "Yes, marriages do often happen later in life, but it's hard to know why Laura didn't marry sooner. Will she now have trouble conceiving and having children?" (p. 140). Mrs. Maken raises a valid concern here. Perhaps the woman she mentions may have a problem getting pregnant. I admit women need to take into account the timespan of their fertility *if they plan to bear children*. Of course, there is no biblical mandate that a married woman must have children (although some have misapplied the Scriptures to make a case to the contrary).

I note that Mrs. Maken fails to acknowledge the alternative for older couples: adoption. If some religionists really believe children are a blessing and that Christian homes have a part in the spread of God's kingdom, what prevents them from exercising this alternative? The act of adoption by devout Christians has the unique advantage in translating a young soul out of an ungodly environment into a godly one. When religionists unduly focus on procreation as the means by which Christian women celebrate motherhood and by which Christian homes are established, they betray a shallow and narcissistic view of family life. In such a case, one must ask if many of the paeans sung to motherhood are merely window-dressing for emotional self-interest. Family isn't about genetics as much as it is about nurture, training, admonition, and love (Eph. 6:4; Titus 2:4).

In essence, I grant there are probably shortcomings to getting married at a later age, but I have already indicated (and Mrs. Maken has conceded) that there are "trade-offs" for many decisions in life. Getting married young poses it own set of challenges. Don't let Mrs. Maken or others fool you into thinking otherwise.

6. *"It's God's will that you are single right now."*

Once again, I agree with Mrs. Maken in rejecting this statement, but for a different reason. Someone who says it's God's will that a given person be married or single is essentially claiming a form of special revelation of which the Bible says nothing. Mrs. Maken declares, "Protracted singleness rarely glorifies God and cannot save you, sanctify you, or justify you in God's eyes" (p. 141). I respond that this is no more true than saying the same thing about marriage. In this regard, one's marital status, per se, has little if anything to do with one's standing before God. It's the grace of our Lord and obedience to his revealed word that ultimately matters.

7. *"There is no shame in being single."*

Obviously, Mrs. Maken doesn't agree with this statement, and obviously I do. Mrs. Maken doesn't say much in response to it in chapter 11, but she does state that being single is an "abnormal state" (p. 142). Indeed, it is so abnormal that by even by conservative estimates, 39% of women aged 30 or over are single.[1] But seriously, I think I can honestly say it is more abnormal for someone to be home-schooled than it is to be single. Is the integrity of an action based upon how "normal" or "abnormal" it is?

8. *"Dating is fun!"*

I agree with Mrs. Maken that many times dating is not fun. Mrs. Maken says it is "unfair to women" (Ibid.). Perhaps it is, although I think some qualifications are in order on that point. At any rate, Mrs. Maken takes this matter up in more detail in the next chapter of her book, and accordingly, the next part of my critique will address what she says there.

PART XIII

Chapter 12
"Saying No to the Dating Game"
(As If Anything Would Change Thereby)

If Debbie Maken were still single, she would probably not be one to go out on dates. She claims in chapter 12 of her book that dating represents "a broken system," and that "it's time to call it quits" (p. 145). Mrs. Maken goes on to spend the rest of the chapter detailing the alleged evils of the modern dating scene. As can be expected, she suggests that women suffer the most in having to date: "Despite the fact that men often resent dating because they have to foot the bill, I believe women pay a much higher price" (Ibid.). Yet is this actually the case? Contrary to Mrs. Maken, I believe there other factors to consider when addressing the challenge men and women face in getting to know each other.

Women Always Have It Worse, Don't Cha Know

If there is any mantra that would best describe the current thinking in our society about gender relations, it would be, "Women always have it worse." This statement lies at the heart of feminism and all the other gynocentrist manifestations of self-pity and entitlement found in our culture. I am afraid that some of the same thinking surfaces in chapter 12 of Mrs. Maken's book. On page 147, she speaks of dating promoting a "lack of equality," as if she were suddenly the champion of downtrodden women everywhere fighting against patriarchy. Mrs. Maken explains her position thusly:

> In its most prevalent form, dating is initiated by men who pursue women for companionship, sex, living together, or marriage. Though many people believe that it's perfectly okay for women to initiate a dating relationship, the simple fact is that most women don't.

> Because that's the way it is, a man has the ultimate balance of power in dating. He looks around at his leisure, decides who he thinks is the most physically and emotionally attractive, and asks her out for a date—all on his timetable. A woman waits for a man to become interested, and when and if

he asks her out, her only power is a decisional one—whether or not to accept his invitation. (p. 147–148)

Who are we kidding, here? Men have the "ultimate balance of power?" How strange that women insist on sharing power with men in every other field of endeavor, but can't seem to want the "power" that men have in initiating relationships. Why is it that we can have female astronauts, politicians, scientists, and lawyers, but we have difficulty getting ladies to ask men out or to pay for dates? Are women who have no problem comporting themselves in an assertive manner and lording their authority over men suddenly worried about their femininity if they ask a man out? Get real.

I think it is obvious that Mrs. Maken is overstating her case here. She opines, "A woman feels pressured into accepting invitations from less than worthy candidates. Her veto power isn't much of a bargaining chip, because the downside of saying no is losing more time until the next offer comes in" (p. 148). Yet, I wonder how many seconds it takes for a woman to say in a polite tone, "I'm sorry but I am not interested. Thanks anyway." Simply put, many women do not have to go through the gut-wrenching anxiety of making the first move. They can signal their interest to a man in ways that provide some safety for their reputations—and their egos.

The same cannot be said for men. Asking the wrong woman out can get a man labeled as a "creep" or a "stalker." Even worse, a man can find himself the target of a frivolous lawsuit or disciplinary action at work. Women have treated men shabbily in this regard. In days gone by, a rejection was nothing more than that—a rejection. Now, a man is forced to navigate an emotional and legal minefield to gain a woman's acceptance, thanks in no small part to feminism and misplaced chivalry. Too many women have been weaned on a diet of misandry, victimhood, hostility, and paranoia. Even their body language betrays a confrontational attitude. Who wants to get up the nerve to ask these kind of women out? Let's face it: Dating is not fun for many men. The whole experience is filled with angst because there is always the fear that a man's advances will be taken the wrong way. From undue public embarrassment to shattered careers, many men are coming to the conclusion that the drama of approaching a woman is not worth it.

With respect to the expenses of dating, Mrs. Maken's position doesn't even make the qualifying round of sound reasoning. It is usually men who are expected to pick up the tab for all social outings with a woman. After men open their wallets, women complain that these gents "expect something" in return. Indeed, men should. At the very least, some integrity and courtesy on the part of the woman is not too much to ask, is it? Somehow, it's perfectly okay for women to send mixed signals about their intentions while men are excoriated for doing the same. I myself have been the casualty of a

Christian woman who was more than willing to let me take her out for dates, only to tell me afterwards that friendship was the best she could offer. Why the sudden change in demeanor? I daresay this happens to men more often than many care to admit.

Is the Man So Beneath You?

Elsewhere in chapter 12, Mrs. Maken writes: "Sally was in her late thirties, owned her own home, and had a respectable job and a decent savings account. She was dating someone who, though older, was a pizza delivery boy. I was shocked. She actually became engaged to this individual, which was even more shocking. At some point she looked up and thought, *This isn't fair*. The engagement ended, and I have to admit I was relieved" (p. 148). I gather that Mrs. Maken finds something undesirable about pizza delivery boys. However, what needs to addressed is the larger problem of how men have been displaced in this society. Since the Industrial Revolution, men have viewed their contribution to their marriage and family largely in terms of the paycheck they bring home from their employers. Now, there is a decrease in manufacturing jobs which typically favor men and an increase in service sector jobs which favor women. On top of this, women are infiltrating high-paying, white-collar jobs traditionally held by men.

What should men do when schools, universities, and workplaces increasingly favor women over them? Men could repeatedly go back to school to acquire more marketable skills, yet in chapter 4, Mrs. Maken bemoans people who spend extended periods of time getting an education. So what man could make it in the brave new world that Mrs. Maken proposes? Obviously, one already born into a position of privilege. This basically is the no-win situation that faces any man who buys into Mrs. Maken's paradigm.

Speaking of pizza delivery boys, I should point out that I have known two grown men who have delivered pizzas to get themselves through school or to support a family. These men are not irresponsible "slackers" as some might suppose, but spiritually-minded individuals who have shown themselves ready to do whatever it takes to get the proverbial job done. I have been blessed to have one of them work for me. Mrs. Maken's comment does no justice to these two individuals and similar hard-working men of modest means.

As for the woman mentioned by Mrs. Maken, it is difficult for me to have sympathy for her. If she was truly in love and truly compatible with the man to whom she was engaged, why did she let her ambitions drive her away from him? If she was just desperate and grasping at whatever attention came her way, why did she fail to make her intentions clear, defrauding an innocent man in the process? It's one thing to state that pizza delivery boys are not one's type. It's another matter to allow a relationship to proceed to an engagement before having the honesty to admit to one's mating preferences.

Mrs. Maken goes on to say: "Women are generally beholden to men for asking them out, and men are indirectly encouraged to seek out women slightly above them. Who's going to stop them? Since prospective suitors know they will not meet a woman's family on the front end, they can take the gamble of aiming high and hope to get lucky. In the past men would not have been so bold because a girl's parents would tell any suitor beneath her to scram" (Ibid.). I am not sure what I should make of this quote. In what way does Mrs. Maken think the women in question are "above" the men that seek them? Are these women richer, more educated, more attractive, more mature, or more spiritual? I think that compatibility between men and women in terms of faith, values, aspirations, personality, and interests are important, but I find any undue stress on social status to be worrisome. Does Mrs. Maken propose a caste system for men and women as is the case in India? I sincerely hope she is not advocating some form of woman-centered elitism and snobbery in this regard.

Oddly enough, Boundless.org (a website I have previously mentioned as being favorable to Mrs. Maken's views) recently published an article about the problem of status-seeking behaviors. It notes that, among other things, a decline of Christianity's influence over Western culture is consonant with a rise of what is called "status anxiety."[1] Given that this is true, I think we can do just fine without having "status anxiety" in terms of who we pick for a mate. People can bloviate all day long about 1 Timothy 5:8 and men being "breadwinners," but as I suggested in part 5 of my critique, 1 Timothy 5:8 was written to both genders. Applying it exclusively to men is a misuse of the Scriptures that ignores both the original grammar and context. Even if I were to grant the misuse of this passage for the sake of argument, the Bible still says:

> Now godliness with contentment is great gain. For we brought nothing into this world, and it is certain we can carry nothing out. *And having food and clothing, with these we shall be content.* But those who desire to be rich fall into temptation and a snare, and into many foolish and harmful lusts which drown men in destruction and perdition. For the love of money is a root of all kinds of evil, for which some have strayed from the faith in their greediness, and pierced themselves through with many sorrows. (1 Tim. 6:6–10) (emphasis mine)

Women should stop having so much anxiety about a man's status, as opposed to considering his character and personal compatibility. Too many of them have forgotten what the Bible *really* says about rating men as being "above" or "beneath" them (Luke 12:15; James 1:9–11; Rom. 12:16; Phil. 2:1–8).

In fact, it's saddening to see how many women are herd creatures in terms of whom they date. Many of them do not pursue relationships with quality men, sometimes not even with men to whom they are initially attracted. Their choice of men is instead largely driven by the approval of their female friends. Men become fashion accessories as a consequence. Needless to say, women must start thinking for themselves, or if they need approval from other women, they ought to seek out the advice of godly and mature women (Titus 2:3–5). When I say mature women, I have in mind ladies who are over the age of 55 and reject the Oprah Winfrey/Dr. Phil/Lifetime Channel culture of female entitlement. Perhaps younger women might be consulted, but sadly in the wake of feminism, there seems to be a lot of women who are just as immature in their thirties and forties as they were in high school.

Dating Doesn't Work - No Kidding, Sherlock

I agree with Debbie Maken that dating, as it often exists, is largely a dysfunctional system for fostering intimate relationships between men and women. Mrs. Maken complains that woman lose their time, trust, innocence, and passion after dating for a long time. She says: "Though a good word of caution, telling women not to put too much of an 'emotional investment' into dating denies our female nature. We're back once more to the fact that God designed us for marriage. It's our nature to want it. And because that's how God made us, that's what we're invariably looking for as we date" (p. 149). The problem is that one does not always detect this "female nature" in young women today. In fact, many women seem to be more in love with their independence, consumer goods, outings with fellow friends, etc. than with any men that come their way. I have lived through a decade of "Girl power" and stupid lifestyle magazine columns emblazoned with the question, "Who Needs Men?" (or with similar revealing titles). How many young men looking for the woman of their dreams were sidelined because a girl was too busy chasing excitement or was shacking up with all the wrong guys? Let's level here: After seeing how many women behave, men also lose their time, trust, innocence, and passion.

Debbie Maken goes on to say that dating causes fatigue and that past a certain point, single women cannot "put on rose-colored glasses when looking at the past" (p. 150). I wonder when dating ceases to be fun for women in this respect. Is it when their biological clocks start winding down? It is at the point when they start aging faster than their male counterparts? Is it when they realize that the dating game is no longer rigged in their favor?

What about those women who have never been able to attract a man? Mrs. Maken remarks, "Today we have a *de facto* spinsterhood, in which random women—many of whom are incredibly beautiful and not overly independent—are still single with no apparent explanation. Singleness is *no longer for the ugly, the cruel, and the indifferent*" (Ibid.) (emphasis mine). I am sure that will make some physically unattractive women feel better ... *not*. How would have Mrs. Maken comforted these unattractive women in an earlier generation? Would she have handed them the same lines about the "Gift of Singleness" that she herself found tiresome as a single woman? Would Mrs. Maken have demanded that men go against biology and look past these women's appearances, even as she and others obviously do not look past the kind of jobs men have (e.g., the "pizza delivery boy")? Would she have declared these women to be predestined to sexual frustration and sin, and perhaps predestined to hell?

Really, why does extended singleness suddenly become a tragedy when "incredibly beautiful" women are passed by? Why do we feel there is "no apparent explanation" to their singleness? Quite frankly, I think there are of plenty of "incredibly beautiful" women who are ignorant, vain, unstable, calculating, materialistic, hypercritical, boorish, or disrespectful to men. It is no mystery to me why many of them are still single. Many of them think they are "too good" for the men around them. Men pick up on this attitude and, accordingly, go to greener pastures where the mares are more prone to nuzzle than kick. Other men just go off and make a stable for themselves.

Old Whine into New Wineskins?

On page 151, Mrs. Maken says that dating forces women to pretend to be disinterested in marriage. I respond that dating forces men to pretend to be disinterested in sex. Either way, no one likes to be around a desperate person. So we'll just have to learn to master our desires, stop acting like other people owe us something in this matter, and be secure in our self-image, won't we? In other words, how do women feel now that the shoe is on other foot? How do they feel now that they are being measured with the same measure that has been used against men?

The way women pressure men into marriage is no more honorable than the way men pressure women into sex. Mrs. Maken remarks, "Of course, men often say they don't know what they're looking for in a wife and that dating someone for a year or two gives them a chance to figure it out" (p. 152). Of course, men say this—because it's true. I am tired of the whining that "men won't commit." Marriage is a more costly proposition for men these days than it was in the past. More is expected from them as husbands and fathers. If a marriage breaks up, they stand to lose more than women. So, it's only natural that a man treads cautiously into the institution of marriage. Who can blame him for wanting to know the woman he is dating well enough before making such a grave decision?

Mrs. Maken continues her tirade about men today who meet their spouses much later in life than men of the past. Supposedly in days gone by, a man tarnished his reputation if he went out with a woman more than three or four times without the intention of marriage. Mrs. Maken thinks that men can now go from one girlfriend to the next because they have no sense of shame (p. 153). So, shall we shame men into marriage? I caution my readers that *shame doesn't work very well when employed by the shameless*. In this sense, many women, religious or otherwise, have comported themselves in a quite a shameless manner for some time. How about returning to shaming women who divorce their husbands for frivolous reasons, single moms, women who knowingly chase rakes, and women who go into male-dominated professions? I suppose that in many respects most people would not want to turn back the clock for women. Fair enough. Yet no matter how you feel about the situation, the proverbial genie is out of the bottle. It's downright idiotic to put the old yoke on the male ox while the female ox gets to roam all over the field. There is going to have to be a monumental sea change of thought in our society before we can go back to the "good old days." Let's not think we can put the old whine (yes, I spelled it that way) into new wineskins.

Just Say No ... As If Others Won't Do the Same to You

At the end of chapter 12, Debbie Maken adjures her readers to "just say no" to the way dating is done. She says that whenever a woman dates a man, the woman should ask about his intentions, motives, and history. Mrs. Maken also says any man who is not serious about getting married should be dumped. Finally, Mrs. Maken advises women to be honest about what they want and set limits (such as breaking off a relationship if it doesn't proceed towards marriage by a certain time).

I suppose this advice is somewhat feasible. Yet I have to ask why dating someone you break up with is necessarily a "waste" of "time"? I think of all the friends I have had during my youth and how many of them have moved on with their lives. Because I am no longer in touch with them, does it mean that the time I enjoyed with them was all for naught? If it wasn't for naught, why should the situation necessarily be different with members of the opposite sex—even with former girlfriends?

When women complain that they "wasted their time" on a man who "won't commit," I think there is usually more than meets the eye. First of all, are these women saying there was no inherent joy or pleasure in the time they spent with their ex-boyfriends? If there was joy, then why automatically call it a "waste of time"? If there wasn't any joy, then were these women just going through the motions to get something out of a man? Like men, women need to be honest about their motivations. Women constantly complain of men who are just being nice in order to "get into" somebody's "pants." Is being nice to a man in order to get his paycheck and have children by him that much more acceptable? If anyone thinks this kind of opportunism is fine for women, remember what the Bible says: "Let love be without hypocrisy" (Rom. 12:9). Indeed, men might have their own questions about the intentions, motivations, and personal history of women.

This is why I insist that a man and woman start with a genuine friendship. The friendship should be reciprocal in terms of trust, respect, and generosity. It should have value in and of itself; it should have no strings attached and no premature expectations of where it will lead. In such a relationship, it's easier for both parties to be honest about their intentions. There is no need to devote exclusive attention to a friend of the opposite sex until there is expressed mutual agreement about the state of the relationship.

Having said that, however, I will say it's difficult to form such a friendship if one has a paranoid attitude about the opposite sex, makes up peculiar rules for "limiting access" to oneself, prematurely asks others pointed and potentially embarrassing questions about their past romantic life—you get the picture. Debbie Maken starts off chapter 12 comparing dating to a job interview where the woman takes the role of the employer. If you are a woman who sees dating in this way, don't be surprised if men treat the prospect of dating you like a job interview as well (and seek women that don't make them feel that way).

Conclusion

Chapter 12 is too much like chapter 4—lopsided in its criticism of men. We are supposed to believe that dating doesn't work and men have an unfair advantage. How strange that after a few generations of dating as we know it, women like Mrs. Maken are only now discovering its shortcomings. Why has there been no similar outcry about men getting shortchanged in dating? I suspect that, as usual, the concerns of average men simply do not matter to many "relationship experts."

There is one final issue that I want to raise about chapter 12 of Mrs. Maken's book. On page 146, Debbie Maken quotes a character from the TV series *Sex in the City* (just as she does in the previous chapter on page 142). I do not know if Mrs. Maken watches the program or if she knows someone else who does, but why are quotations from a ribald program aired on HBO supposed to carry weight with a Christian readership? I know many men who find *Sex in the City* to be disgusting in its celebration of contemporary vice, especially as displayed by secular women. The fact that Mrs. Maken quotes from this program causes me some concern. The fact that her publisher, literary agent, reviewers, etc. did not dissuade her from doing so causes me some concern. Forgive me if I sound alarmist, but I wonder what the state of biblical womanhood is in this culture when we see religious women looking to worldly female characters on a sitcom for literary inspiration. Surely, people can do better than this.

PART XIV

Chapter 13
"Enlisting Agency"
(And Playing Hard to Get)

In my review of chapter 12 of Debbie Maken's book, *Getting Serious about Getting Married*, I noted that Mrs. Maken rejects common approaches to dating. In chapter 13 of her book, however, she proposes an alternative system of courtship (or dating) via enlisted agency. Specifically, Mrs. Maken wants parents to be more actively involved in finding a spouse for their daughters and in warding off undesirable suitors. Mrs. Maken believes enlisted agency will cause men to be more accountable to women, increase the likelihood of women meeting quality men, and reduce the heartbreak of failed relationships. There are, unsurprisingly, many assumptions put forth in chapter 13 of Mrs. Maken's book that deserve a good measure of scrutiny.

Israelites in Love

There is a fad among many Evangelicals to push a "pattern" of "biblical dating" (i.e., courtship) which supposedly has support in the Scriptures. Mrs. Maken is no exception in this regard. Like many other pundits, she goes back to the Old Testament and presumes that it furnishes a suitable model for how Christians should find their spouses today. I find it ironic though that Mrs. Maken and others can find no meaningful support from the New Testament, the spiritual covenant to which Christians are bound (Heb. 8:1–13). They cannot even find enough commandments given by God to the Israelites. Rather, their model of courtship essentially rests on incidental biblical narratives and certain exegetical penumbras (including fanciful inferences drawn from figurative language).

Consider Mrs. Maken's treatment of Abraham as a case in point. She claims that Abraham was initially neglectful of his duty to find a wife for Isaac but later fulfilled his duty when he realized that Isaac was lonely and needed a spouse (pp. 157–158). Yet the text doesn't say Abraham was neglectful in getting Isaac a wife. That is Mrs. Maken's addition to the passage. Moreover, the text doesn't say Abraham felt pity because of Isaac's loneliness or that Abraham was some firm believer in the "marriage mandate," per se. We need not conjecture about Abraham's motives. The

Scriptures already furnish us with a valid reason for Abraham's attempt to find a wife from his home country for Isaac: "The LORD God of heaven, *who took me from my father's house and from the land of my family, and who spoke to me and swore to me, saying, 'To your descendants I give this land,'* He will send His angel before you, and you shall take a wife for my son from there" (Gen. 24:7; see also Gen. 17:15–21) (emphasis mine). In other words, Abraham wanted to make sure God's promise through Isaac would come to pass. Here is something else to note about this narrative: It proves the courtship advocates to be inconsistent in their use of the Scriptures. They often insist that a male suitor must initiate a relationship with a female, but Isaac didn't do this. A wife was brought to him by a servant. On top of this, Isaac was forty-years old when he married (Gen. 25:20). Nothing in the Scriptures indicates God's displeasure either with Isaac or with Abraham about such a late marriage; on the contrary, God seems to be been quite pleased with the way Abraham comported himself (Gen. 24:1b). This flies in the face of those such as Mrs. Maken who would shame young men into seeking marriage. Indeed, how does the phrase "wife of thy youth" apply to Isaac?

Debbie Maken's exegesis also fails to acknowledge the historical and culture milieu of the Scriptures she cites. Mrs. Maken says, "Rebekah was under the protective covering of her parents, uncle, or clan. They were the ones making sure she was entering into a safe union" (p. 158). I grant that many Old Testament fathers probably felt protective towards their daughters. Yet we must also remember that in the nomadic societies of that time, women were considered to be subject to the authority of their fathers or any older male siblings in forming a marriage contract.[1] We see this clearly in Laban's involvement in the negotiations for his sister's marriage (Gen. 24:28–61).

Mrs. Maken also says, "Abraham's agent knew he had to prove Isaac's worthiness and success to get Rebekah's family to agree to the match. Thus the flashy caravan and costly gifts" (p. 159). In actuality, the servant proved the worth of the *household into which Rebekah would enter*. Keep in mind that the goods shown to Rebekah ultimately came from Abraham's wealth, not Isaac's. It should not surprise us to see Abraham acting on Isaac's behalf, because unlike many modern households, the Old Testament patriarchs lived in extended families.[2] Mrs. Maken asserts, "The Genesis model of marriage intimates that the perfect pattern is for both the man and woman to leave their respective homes to make a new home together" (p. 163), but we see that such is not necessarily the case in the Bible.

The gifts to Rebekahs' family were not just to prove the worth of Abraham's household, either; they constituted a price that had to be paid to the bride's family. This was the costume of the times. A woman was given to a male suitor in exchange for goods or services. This also explains Jacob agreeing to work seven years for Laban in return for obtaining Rachel as a wife (Gen. 29:18), an arrangement in which Jacob was considered to be part of Laban's household (Gen. 31:41).[3]

As with the Patriarchs, Mrs. Maken misses the mark on the story of Ruth. Mrs. Maken thinks that Ruth going to a threshing floor in the middle of the night to solicit Boaz's favor was dangerous and unwise and that it represents the unfortunate result of there not being a male agency to act on behalf of Ruth (p. 160). With respect to what Ruth did, we may question the wisdom of her coming to Boaz in the middle of the night, but there is one thing that Debbie Maken and other modern courtship advocates cannot do: question Ruth's initiative as a woman. Boaz did not say to Ruth, "Your proposing marriage to me is unladylike!" No, he extols her as a righteous woman with a reasonable request even after what she did (Ruth 3:10–11). The Scriptures do not condemn Ruth's behavior or any "passivity" or "lack of leadership" on the part of Boaz. We cannot but conclude that in the absence of familial authority, women are not obligated to be passive in dating and courtship.

This brings me to my next point: The way Debbie Maken and so many commentators treat the Scriptures reminds me of the Sunday crowds in family-style buffet restaurants. The restaurant crowds pick up a plate, mosey up to the pans filled with various foodstuffs, and pick whatever they want. If they don't like broccoli or spinach salad, they can move on and pile their plates full of fried chicken and mashed potatoes. Likewise, some warm up to the idea of a family member acting as a dating agency for them, men having to take initiative in approaching women, men not being able to interact with women unless they want to court for marriage, and men having to bestow gifts and make demonstrations of their financial success before they can spend any time with a woman. They may gleefully point to the Scriptures to make these things imperative. What many of these same individuals won't do is champion the notion of women being stripped of legal rights or social mobility; grown women having to answer to a father, much less a male sibling; or women having to live in extended families with in-laws. Yet these latter details are just as much a part of the Biblical narrative as the other ones.

Mrs. Maken can wax eloquent all day long abut how, in former times, familial agency limited the access men had to women, but she fails to acknowledge that it worked the other way as well—women's access to men was limited by their families. Family agency doesn't sound so wonderful when your relatives ward off someone you *want* to marry. And it doesn't sound appealing if you're an adult woman who cannot make decisions about your life because you are forced to live at home with your parents, even though Mrs. Maken recommends women do this very thing (p. 163). In the past, there were plenty of stories about women who married or even eloped just to get out of their parent's house and who ended up jumping from the proverbial frying pan into the fire. Let's not kid ourselves and look at days gone by through rose-colored lenses.

There also some things about the Old Testament that are an outright embarrassment to modern courtship advocates. In the Patriarchal age, marriage was about the consolidation of property. Bloodlines had to be established and a man had to ensure that his children were indeed related to him; male heirs were of primary importance.[4] As for women, a great deal of emphasis was placed on their reproductive capacities. For instance, we see in the Old Testament narratives that when women were barren, they gave their handmaids to their husbands by which to sire children (Gen. 16:1–3; Gen. 30:1–13). We also see that much is said about a woman's virginity in the Old Testament, but nothing regarding the virginity of a man, who could have multiple wives, concubines, etc. and still be declared righteous in God's sight.

I am certain modern courtship advocates can find plenty of scriptural reasons to explain away polygamy and the looser sexual mores of the Old Testament. However, they will have some difficulty explaining away levirate marriages as a requirement (Gen. 38:8; Deut. 25:5); the treatment of women's sexuality as family property that can bartered away, even in cases of rape (Deut. 22:28–29); or endogamy (Gen. 24: 4) which would be required in some instances (Num. 36:1–13). Of course, such things present no problem to the rest of us who don't waste time trying to salvage Old Testament customs as a pattern for how Christians should date and marry (Heb. 8:1–13).

Other Exegetical Mishaps by Courtship Advocates

Courtship advocates also misuse other scriptures to justify their pattern of "biblical dating," especially to insist that men must take initiative in finding a spouse. For instance, many of them argue that men must initiate a relationship with a woman because Christ did the same for the Church. In part 10 of my critique, I briefly touched upon the egregious error commentators make in assuming a one-for-one correspondence between a literal human marriage and the figurative marriage between God and his people. The matrimonial language used in the Bible to describe God and his people is metaphorical, not typological. Such language has a limited context and therefore a limited application. Indeed, I don't see too many courtship advocates affirming the right of a man to take vengeance on a woman who rejects him the way God will take vengeance on those who reject their Creator. Nor do I see people arguing that Christ is dependent upon the Church as a "helpmeet" the way some think men need women. Let's suppose I am wrong and that Christ's relationship with the Church represents an all-encompassing pattern for how men are to relate to women. Even so, we would still have to grapple with those scriptures that admonish people to initiate a relationship with God, not the other way around (Ps. 119:2; Heb. 11:6; Acts 17:24–27).

Apart from misusing figurative language in the Bible, courtship advocates often use Proverbs 18:22 as a key proof-text: "He who finds a wife finds a good thing, and obtains favor from the Lord." Many assume this passage requires a man to do all the legwork in establishing a relationship with a woman. However, the passage is not a commandment but a general statement that one will be blessed in having a wife, a promise which is not guaranteed in all cases (Prov. 12:4b). Moreover, the verb in this passage is "to find," not "to seek"; clearly, the stress is laid on the happenstance of obtaining a good thing, not in the effort expended to pursue it.[5] Finally, there is no reason to limit the application of this passage to just one sex. I note that courtship advocates do not restrict the application of passages like Matthew 5:27–30 and Matthew 19:9 just to men. If women can be guilty of mental adultery like men, or if they can divorce and remarry for scriptural reasons like men, then surely they can blessed in finding husbands just as men can be blessed in finding wives.

Sometimes, those who dispense rules on dating go to hilarious extremes in their misapplication of the Scriptures. Consider this example from the Boundless.org website:

> Genesis 2:22 tells us that after God made Eve, he brought her to Adam. Now what we might have expected next was for God to say something: explain the purpose of marriage, assure Adam that after all the disappointment of not finding a suitable helper (2:19–20), here she was, encourage him about her willingness to marry. But God doesn't do any of that. He simply brings her to Adam and says nothing. The silence is deafening. The next move is all up to him.
>
> What does Adam do? He doesn't flirt with her. He doesn't ask her if she likes him. Instead, he shoulders the risk, steps up to the plate, and declares his intentions for the relationship. When Adam says in Genesis 2:23, "This at last is bone of my bones and flesh of my flesh," he's not just describing where she came from. And he's certainly not flirting, or putting out feelers. He's laying it on the line and declaring his intentions for marriage.[6]

Don't make me laugh. The story of Adam and Eve is *anything but* an example of a relationship that many marriage mandators and courtship advocates promote. Adam did not decide one day that he was getting up in the years and had to "get serious about finding a wife." He did not look high and low to find a spouse. He did not ask God's permission to court Eve. He did not go through some silly process of "defining the relationship" (a concept bandied about by many courtship advocates). In fact, the relationship was already defined by the Almighty: "I will make him a helper comparable to him" (Gen. 2:18). What was left for Adam to do? The only thing he could do was acknowledge Eve as his wife ("bone of my bones and flesh of my flesh"). If anything is to be carried away from this story, it is how far humanity has drifted in what it expects of men who would marry.

Most of our current expectations of men, no matter how biblical they are, are at best remedial; they do not reflect the ideal of Eden. In fact, many expectations are not even biblical at all, but cultural. We do well if we realize our expectations for what they are. We may balk at the idea of women asking men out for dates, but it was not too long ago that many balked at the idea of women wearing slacks or working in jobs traditionally held by men. Gender roles are not as static as we like to think they are. Many of us no longer live in nomadic societies or even agrarian ones. While the Bible is a necessary guide in how men and women should act, we need to avoid the kind of exegetical train wrecks in slow motion that seem to occur in the camp of the neo-traditionalists. Let's not misuse the Bible to justify our social and cultural biases.

A Covering for Women or Just a Cover-Up?

One recurrent theme throughout chapter 13 of Debbie Maken's book is that women are especially vulnerable in the arena of dating and courtship and are in need of a "covering." I suppose such protection made sense when women's opportunities were limited. But now women insist on being thought of as men's equals in so many endeavors. From what, therefore, do women need protection? Is it the consequences of their actions? If women are not adult enough to handle these consequences, then why should we allow women a place of prominence in society or maintain that they have a right to the same opportunities as men? Mrs. Maken recommends using a "strong agent" such as a father to act as a mediator in the courtship process. But if a woman needs a father to vet calls from male suitors, does she also need one to vet calls from male employers or colleagues? Part of adulthood is realizing that privileges come with responsibilities. Many women to need grow up in that regard and stop asking for preferential treatment when it suits their fancy.

To be honest, the only thing I think we are protecting is the inflated ego a woman might have. On page 169, Mrs. Maken notes, "The number one complaint of women in college today is that men no longer ask them out for dates." Why don't these women take a little initiative themselves? I suppose the prospect of asking a man out is unappealing to them because they fear rejection. In this regard, they seem more than happy to turn the matter over men. Suddenly, all the bravado about "Girl power," "breaking through glass ceilings," "beating the boys," etc. flies out the window and we find women tying themselves to the railroad tracks, crying out for Dudley Do-right. If a woman doesn't get asked out for a date, she can reason that men don't have a proper respect for a "biblical mandate to lead" or that men are "not serious about marriage." If she asks a man out and gets rejected, she comes face-to-face with the reality that Madison Avenue, Hollywood, and the family bookstore haven't been exactly truthful about today's woman being smart, beautiful, and God's gift to men.

Rapunzel in a Six-Foot High Tower

Let's go further and ask ourselves just what problems is enlisted agency supposed to solve for women? Mrs. Maken's believes that the unlimited access men have to women dulls any sense of urgency men may have about marrying. Mrs. Maken claims, "Every function normally associated with a wife has been fragmented: food comes from take-out, sex comes from just about anywhere (for those who disregard God's moral prohibitions), and companionship comes from friends and coworkers" (p. 164). Later she remarks: "This is the core of protracted singleness: Some men who should have been trusted the least now bear the responsibility for making marriage transpire. We must take back responsibility and encourage fathers to take the initiative to find suitable husbands for their daughters" (p. 166). So how does asking your father to play the rottweiler on the front porch mitigate against men enjoying take-out food and the company of friends and coworkers? In other words, what compels a single man to give up the comforts of bachelorhood to face the drama of courting someone who props up the value of her own company through artificial scarcity? Consider this quote:

> Alas, when people complain of men not marrying (even they who are able), they forget how little women offer in exchange for all they get by marriage. Girls are so seldom taught to be of any use whatever to a man that I am only astonished at the numbers of men who do marry! Many girls do not even try to be agreeable to look at, much less to live with. They forget how numerous they are, and the small absolute need men have of wives; but, nevertheless, men do still marry, and would oftener marry could they find mates—women who are either helpful to them, or amusing, or pleasing to their eye.[7]

Was this penned by some cranky bachelor on the Internet? No. This is an excerpt of a self-improvement book written by a woman for women in 1878! I cannot but infer that men have been reticent to marry even in an age of courtship and strict sexual mores. If men weren't necessarily dying to tie the knot with women in 1878, it's certainly not surprising men are even more hesitant to marry today in the wake of feminism, gynocentrism in popular culture, and technologies which liberate men from needing someone to do domestic chores.

Apart from what men did in bygone days of courtship, what shall we say about the current practice of dating? What inferences can we draw from

Debbie Maken's assertion on page 161 that our modern dating system came from the 1920s? Surely if the current practice of dating has been a problem, then we should have seen a precipitous decline of marriages in the 1920s or a few decades afterwards. But we don't see that when we look at the numbers. In actuality, apart from the Depression Era, the rate of women marrying rose until the 1940s and declined sharply in the 1970s.[8] Mrs. Maken has overstated her case in pointing the finger at modern dating as the cause of the single woman's woes. A more likely explanation for the decline in marriage is a shrinking middle class[9] and the disruption of traditional gender roles.

At any rate, I believe Mrs. Maken reveals something about the mind of the typical contemporary woman:

> If a woman wants to be a lawyer, she can go to law school, take the Bar Exam, send out resumés to employers, and practice law. If a woman wants to run for office, she can put her name in the hat, run a good election campaign, and win the race. If a woman wants to travel to Australia, she can buy airline tickets, pack her bags, and go. In other words, she can do something to accomplish her goals. But if she wants to get married, she's told to sit like a bump on a log until the right Christian man finds her. I don't think so. (p. 165)

I have to admire Mrs. Maken for encouraging initiative in women, but how does using parental intermediaries address the problem of Christian women sitting like bumps on the log? Apparently, some women think they can push a button and make their dream husband appear the way they push buttons on a microwave, TV remote, cell phone, or iPod and get results. In the wake of expanded opportunities for women, it may be quite a shock for some of them to realize a man can actually deny them an opportunity and get away with it. No government program or grassroots movement can force men to love women. So before Mrs. Maken and her fans talk about "enlisting agency," maybe they should discuss how to get men to be interested in the first place.

From page 166 to 167 of her book, Debbie Maken discuss how using agency worked for her. In her own case, she employed the services of an Indian website: "Through this agency, I first met my future mother-in-law. She was searching for a wife for her son, who also had a legal background. Once again, the Indian culture more closely resembles how culture in America and Europe used to be: Mothers are actively involved in finding mates for their children. Even though the custom would have been for my parents to write to them, I wrote to her myself, and she and my future father-in-law were so impressed that they asked their son to correspond with me. And the rest is history" (p. 167). I am quite amused by this account of Mrs. Maken's courtship. Throughout her book she takes a firm stance on male leadership, and as we have noted in the chapter under consideration, she calls for "father figures" to acts as agents in behalf of marriageable women. However, we see that Mrs. Maken's own guidelines don't seem apply to her marriage. The very example of her own personal situation does not support her case, but undermines it. What we have instead is an example of two women taking initiative: one in behalf of her son, and one in finding a husband. What has "worked" for Mrs. Maken is dropping the trappings of female passivity, at least in the search for a spouse. This leads me back to Mrs. Maken's remark about women being able to find jobs, hold positions of power, be mobile, etc. and yet not being able to find a husband. Agency may work some in ferreting out irresponsible men, but to find the committed ones, women may have to get off their sofas and seek out Prince Charming—just as Mrs. Maken did.

One Size Doesn't Fit All

Courtship guidelines are like designer jeans—one size doesn't fit all. We can all congratulate Mrs. Maken for her success in finding a spouse. I certainly wish the best for her marriage. All the same, what has worked for her may not work for someone else. She ignores the serious challenges that face men and women in the courtship game, challenges that are not remedied by adding rules and referees.

In my review of chapter 12, I mentioned women who complain about lost time spent on men who won't commit. In response to these women, I would counter that condemning single Christian men as heartless players who jump from one girlfriend to the next is neither an honest nor helpful approach. There are other reasons why a relationship with a man may not pan out for a woman. Here are a few that come to mind:

1. Christian women date non-Christian men and make themselves vulnerable. They then blame all men for the behavior of those fellows who should have been avoided in the first place.

2. One party in a relationship may presume too much about where the relationship is headed and may not be straightforward about his or her expectations of the other party.

3. The man is not afraid of commitment but is intimidated by the high expectations a woman may have of him. He may turn his back on a given relationship to find someone else who is more realistic about what a relationship should entail.

4. The man senses that he is not really appreciated for who he is and that he is just a tool for the ambitions of the woman he is dating or courting.

5. The initial attraction faded and now there is no commonality between the parties in a relationship. Both parties did not bother to form a friendship before dating or courting, so they are left with the awkward remains of a fizzled romance.

6. One party realized after a while that the other party was simply not right for him or her in some other way.

Debbie Maken's model of courtship will not make these problems go away or keep a woman's time from being "wasted" on a relationship that doesn't lead to marriage.

Mrs. Maken's suggested schedule for moving a couple towards marriage is not helpful either. She says on page 175, "Personally, I think two dates are more than enough to scratch someone off the list, and I would suggest three months is ample time to elicit a proposal." Where did she come up with this hard and fast rule? What premarital counseling experts did she consult? I do not believe three months is a long enough time to get a sense for who a person really is. This is especially the case if one's access to the other party is limited by distance, schedules ... or courtship rules.

Another troublesome matter is Mrs. Maken's reference to 1 Corinthians 7:36 as proof that fathers "are required to actively seek a marriage estate for their daughters" (p. 164). She earlier asserts on page 41 that the following verse (v. 37) applies to unmarried people. Both verses, in actuality, are addressed to the *same* individuals. If we follow Mrs. Maken view on verse 36, then we are forced to conclude from verse 37 that fathers have a right to *forbid* their daughters from marrying. I don't think Mrs. Maken would take that position, but she nonetheless shoots herself in the foot by failing to think through her arguments carefully enough. It is simply not wise to take scriptures out of context to make a requirement about enlisted agency.

Playing Hardball by Playing Hard to Get

I have touched upon how the use of enlisted agency does not guarantee the kind of successful outcomes that Debbie Maken promises, but I want to make some additional comments about Mr. Mrs. Maken's notion that the access men have to women should be limited. Consider what she writes at the outset of chapter 13: "*I am proposing that limited and guarded access to women produces responsible, wise, and efficient decision-making from men, while unlimited and unchecked access produces complacency and generally unwise behavior—exactly where we are today.* Anything that is too widely available is generally thought of as invaluable [sic]. Think about fashion trends. The latest things sported by celebrities is only popular when it's hard to get" (p. 157) (emphasis orig.). What a revealing quote. Why should women play hard to get? Because they want to protect their purity or because they are judicious in their choice of suitors? Well, Mrs. Maken says that a woman should do so because it inflates her value. Would this explain the manipulative behavior of many women? Do they have such a poor image of themselves that they believe the only way they can find a mate is by pretending that they are unapproachable? I wonder how much security and trust these women can have in their marriages when their husbands see them for what they truly are on a daily basis. Or maybe they don't care what their husbands think. I thought the way to increase one's desirability as a wife was by being a woman that demonstrates affection, interest, concern, and respect for a man. But apparently, Mrs. Maken feels that acting guarded and aloof is the way to a man's heart: "If we want men to pursue us, they must feel alone and use that loneliness as an impetus to seek us out. When access to women is limited, men have the glory of having accomplished something by fighting for it or working for it. Their very nature and desire for conquest resists having someone who came too easily" (p. 170).

Mrs. Maken does not know men as well as she think she does. Most men I know hate drama and head games. Women don't do men any favors by being difficult to approach, and any barriers a woman places in the way of a relationship really only serves her agenda. Besides that, why should we presume that Mrs. Maken's advice is going to make much difference when many men already have their access to women limited in other ways? It is limited by feminism and its attendant attitude of androphobia. It is limited by women snubbing decent men left and right in a chase after the banal and superficial things of this life. It is limited by women with ridiculous, unrealistic standards for whom they will marry. It is limited by women being so self-absorbed that they never stop to consider the existence of male human beings around them.

Mrs. Maken wants men to "feel alone" but some men find that even marriage doesn't change that feeling. There are married men who live in emotional isolation because their wives won't allow them to be open about their desires, dreams, fears, doubts, vulnerabilities, and human quirks. They are sadly confined to live up to some cardboard ideal of manhood that their wives have embraced. As for single men, more than enough of them have had plenty of time to adjust to the feeling of being alone. In fact, once these men discover that being single won't kill them and that they can live fulfilling lives without a wedding band on their finger, they no longer behave in a desperate manner around women. Not all single men come to this form of contentment, but those that don't are prisoners of their own device.

As it is, if women can limit the access men have to them, then perhaps men should do the same to women. Mrs. Maken says the following about her courtship guidelines: "I'm not fighting against romance; I am fighting against what I call reckless romanticism, the kind of romanticism where we think we will be overjoyed with spontaneous surprises, one after the other" (p. 169). Since she is a pragmatist, then neither she nor her fans should fault me for being too pragmatic or unromantic in my advice to men:

1. *'Limit access" to your wallet*: Men should not be obligated to pay for dates, especially at the beginning of a relationship. Some women may think that a man demonstrates his ability "to provide" by picking up the tab on dates. But how does a woman demonstrate her ability to be a wife and mother? Surely it isn't done by just coming to the front door looking pretty. If a man pays for a date on Friday, does his girlfriend cook for him on Saturday—or clean his apartment? Why should a man be constantly spending cash on a woman to whom he is neither engaged nor married? Indeed, given the attitude of many women, there is very little difference between dating them and hiring an escort for a social event. There is nothing wrong with splitting expenses or asking for separate checks on a date. Women should be open to the possibility, or at least they should demonstrate in some other tangible way that they know how to be giving individuals.

2. *Determine if her "intentions are honorable"*: A man should probe the motivations of the woman in which he interested. Is she the kind of the person who will take *him* for *better or for worse*, in *sickness or in health*, and for *richer or for poorer*? Or is she just looking for a walking ATM—a male cardboard prop to fit in her dollhouse life of white picket fences, over-sized vehicles, and pretty children?

3. *Determine if she is "serious about marriage"*: Since women are notorious for initiating no-fault divorces, a man might want to consider a prenuptial contract. I understand that the some find this idea to be in poor taste, but if a woman has a right to protect herself from being defrauded before a marriage, a man has a right to the same after a marriage. At the very least, a couple should look into the possibility of a "covenant marriage." Someone might counter that men are the ones who to need to face danger and take risks. The Bible, however, does not counsel men to take risks with unscrupulous women (Prov. 21:19; Eccl. 7:26). A man has a right to throw out the bad apples the way women have. In short, when it comes to issues of trust, whatever measure a woman may use against men should be measured back to her. Fairness demands no less (Matt. 7:1–2).

More of the Same

I conclude my review of chapter 13 by noting that, like previous chapters, it contains some sexist assumptions about men that truly need to be challenged. For instance, Mrs. Maken opines that her courtship system will "tame men to behave like men" (p. 143). This assertion reminds me of George Gilder and other socially conservative pundits who advance the idea that women have a civilizing effect on men. It's a spurious notion that was aptly branded and exposed as the "Gilder Fallacy" by Daniel Amneus in his book, *The Garbage Generation*, years ago. Amneus made this observation: "The key issue is not, as Gilder imagines, whether men can be induced to accept the Sexual Constitution which he imagines women try to impose, but whether women themselves can be induced to accept it."[10] Despite what Debbie Maken might think, women need to tame themselves before thinking about taming men.

Mrs. Maken's sexist assumptions also include some double-standards. In one statement in chapter 13, she mentions men who "cannot (or will not) make up their mind" about women on online dating sites (p. 172). She, of course, fails to acknowledge women who are also guilty in this regard, especially in light of their attention-seeking behaviors. Then there is this elitist remark from Mrs. Maken: "We often silently wonder, *How did he get her?* when we see an average, ho-hum kind of man with an outstanding woman. Rarely do we question how *she* got *him*. There aren't that many cocktail waitresses married to brain surgeons" (p. 173) (emphasis orig.). I suspect, however, that the reason people don't wonder about how women get lucky is because they take the hypergamous behavior of women for granted, cocktail waitresses or no cocktail waitresses. I think this also explains Mrs. Maken dig at men "delivering pizzas at thirty-eight" (Ibid.).

In essence, whatever positives that could be gleaned from chapter 13 of Mrs. Maken's book are outweighed by wrong-headed assumptions about women, men, courtship, and the Bible itself. I will also note that as bad as this chapter is in its treatment of men, the last full chapter of her book is even worse. It is to that part of her book that I will next turn my attention.

PART XV

Chapter 14
"Inspiring Men to Biblical Manhood"
(The Final Solution)

In chapter 14 of Debbie Maken's book, she offers some suggestions that supposedly will inspire Christian men to heed the call of marriage. Yet instead of giving one a reason to find hope in a largely anti-male and anti-family society, chapter 14 sadly mimics chapter 4 in its harangue against single men. With that in mind, I will now slog through some of Mrs. Maken's short-sighted observations about those of my gender.

Real Leadership or Romance Novel Leadership?

Near the beginning of chapter 14, Debbie Maken declares, "God made men to be leaders—to pursue marriage and to seek a wife to ease their loneliness" (p. 180). Statements like this one have caused me to reflect on the subtext of this and other calls by religious pundits for men to "lead." What do so many people (especially women) mean by "leadership"? I fear that there is a disconnect between the leadership to which God calls men and the "leadership" that many women want from men. One could say that the former is best termed as "real leadership" and the latter as "romance novel leadership." What separates the two? The first can be seen through the prism of clear scriptural teachings from the New Testament. The second only through a kaleidoscope of misapplied scriptures, cultural biases, gynocentrism, and emotionalism.

So many Christian women are more than eager to compare the husband's role to the role that Christ assumes with regard to the Church. They do so in ways that go well beyond what passages like Ephesians 5:25–33 imply and thus well beyond what is appropriate for any human being to expect from another. Since these Christian women profess a typological view of marriage that mirrors the Christian's relationship to God, it reveals something about their spirituality. Let me suggest that many Christian women want a watered-down form of "leadership" wherein all the privileges accrue to the woman and all the responsibilities accrue to the man. The mindset of these women, in turn, suggests a view of God wherein he is an unassuming deity who dispenses favors and offers protection while asking for little if any sacrifice at all.

With regard to male leadership in the home, I wonder how many contemporary Christian women are willing to accept the idea that in matters of expediency, their judgments are subordinate to a man's? Can one talk of "equal partnership" and men having "leadership" in the same breath? When we look at 1 Timothy 3:4–5, we see that husbands not only lead, they *rule* their household. If men are supposed rule their household, aren't women supposed to *obey* (1 Peter 3:1–6)? A Christian woman is blessed to be married to man who is considerate about her feelings. Yet even in the best circumstances, there will be some disagreements that can only be settled by deferring to one party in a dispute. Will women honor their husbands or maintain a grudge and grow bitter towards them? I have some real concerns about young Christian women raised in the wake of feminism and their ability to truly understand what "biblical leadership" on the part of a husband entails. We are skating on thin ice when we equate "biblical leadership" when how much money a man makes, asking women out on dates, and other cultural norms, while forgetting or downplaying clear biblical teachings that may in fact be uncomfortable for some women to accept.

Another matter to consider is whether or not Christian women really want to revert back to the notions that previous generations had about male leadership. If so, will they go back to the station appointed to them by cultures of a bygone age? Will they give up their legal and social rights? Will they retreat from the spheres of influence over which men once held exclusive sway? Will they accept the charge that berating male suitors about their singleness is unladylike? Will they accept the legal right of men to chastise insubordinate and wayward women? I suspect most Christian women would take exception to such treatment. Yet some still demand that we revive the attitude previous generations had towards single men. Sorry, but this inconsistent thinking doesn't wash.

So many Christian women do not want the kind of leadership that gives a man palpable authority and that demands sacrifice and obedience from a woman. What they want is a kind of "leadership" where men are called upon to the do the heavy-lifting of adult responsibilities while women get to play Martha Stewart. This is why men need to be very discerning when women start talking about men needing to "lead." A man has to separate between genuine, godly women who understand what a husband's role is and those women taken captive by self-contradictory, neo-traditionalist ideas of manhood. I say all of this to make this point: Women need to get off the fence and be consistent. If they want men to lead then they must give up some of the advances they have enjoyed as a result of feminism and modernity. Otherwise, they need to realize responsibilities come with the perks and privileges of contemporary adulthood. This would imply shouldering some of the burdens that men have had to bear for generations. If they refuse to do this, then they judge themselves to be self-serving and not marriage material. It is simple as that.

Let me also note that real male leadership knows when to draw the line in the sand. It means having the courage to say "No" to women if need be. I believe men who balk at Debbie Maken's shaming tactics qualify as "real men" in this regard. Are we to believe that religious men of days gone by would sit passively while women acted like a bunch of scolds, berating men? I don't.

Going to Restaurants and Grilling the Prize Catch

With regard to Debbie Maken's views of male leadership, let us consider how Mrs. Maken and some of her friends have treated men. She says, "I would often tell men I dated that because they were over thirty and still unmarried, they lacked biblical leadership that requires securing a wife. They should have to explain why they are still single" (p. 185) . She then brings up examples where friends of hers either interrogated or rejected older bachelors because these men did not pursue marriage sooner. Mrs. Maken concludes that with respect to single men, people "need to start thinking in terms of godly accountability, not open-ended mercy" (Ibid.). Perhaps men will not run out of a restaurant if they are subjected to the kind of inquisition that Debbie Maken extols. I suppose many men are simply conditioned to sit like inanimate chunks of rock, stoically acquiescing to whatever verbal abuse women heap on them. If the genders were reversed and a man was behaving the way Debbie Maken's friends have behaved, he would be probably have a glass of water thrown in his face. A lot of woman simply have no idea how rude and insensitive they can be.

As it is, I am left wondering what Debbie Maken thinks women can achieve by giving men the third-degree. In my estimation, warding off older single men in the way Mrs. Maken proposes amounts to little more than a Pyrrhic victory. Women over the age of thirty can ill afford to harbor suspicious attitudes towards their male contemporaries. What are these women thinking? Do they think that if they eliminate older single men as "cads" there will still be some men left over? Which men? Younger single men? Wouldn't chasing them be taking husbands away from younger single women? Mrs. Maken's attitude is basically a classic example of what the economist Thomas Sowell would call "stage one thinking," a mindset that fails the acknowledge the consequences of what it proposes.

In addition, noticeably absent from Debbie Maken's equation is any accountability for older single women. Let us rephrase Debbie Maken's words by reversing the genders and circumstances: "I would often tell *women I date* that because they were over thirty and still unmarried, they lack *biblical submissiveness, a quiet spirit, genuine spirituality, and inward beauty* that *attracts and secures a husband.* They should have to explain why they are still single." It sounds harsh, doesn't it? And yet, ironically, it is true about many women in this culture. Do we really believe that pushy, catty, status-seeking, materialist, crypto-feminist women with fading looks, ticking biological clocks, and a bad attitude about men are going to attract suitors left and right just because they get a little religion? Clearly, not all women fit this bill, but too many do. Mrs. Maken, of course, fails to acknowledge this fact. For her to do so would certainly not go over well with her readership of single women who are hopelessly stuck in the mode of faultfinding. Rather, it is easier to conduct a witch hunt against older bachelors, conveniently forgetting the barriers that society and women raise against those men who aspire to marry young.

Shut Up, Buddy, and Sire My Babies

What is ironic about Mrs. Maken's attitude that even though she is fond of demanding accountability from men and limiting the access they have to women, she still says: "Ultimately there are no sound reasons or legitimate excuses why men—especially Christian men—are not getting married. Whatever the excuse *du jour*—lousy parents, divorced parents, protracted educational requirements, the high cost of living, fear of failure, misunderstanding the opposite sex—every excuse to put off marriage is a decision to stay single. Without accountability, nothing will change" (p. 181). Really? This statement is unfortunate. I imagine some women will come away from it, emboldened with the following attitude: "I am not going to worry my pretty little head about the things that menfolk have to go through. They have a job to perform for us ladies and that's that." Yet when a woman shows a cavalier disregard for the problems that men face in this society, it says something about her as a prospective mate. If a woman refuses to show compassion or consideration for men before she marries, how will she act after she is married? Can such a woman truly be a source of emotional support and inspiration? Can she truly be a helpmate? Can she truly say that she knows how to compromise and be submissive when she makes up her mind in advance not to listen to what men are saying? Is stubborn pride a delightful attribute in women, let alone anyone else?

Ironically, with regard to female attributes, Mrs. Maken thinks she has a clue about what kind of women are desirable to men. She states: "If we want men to reach their full biblical potential, we should strive for the same. I think most men are searching for women who are smart, intelligent, good conversationalists, intriguing, educated, able to speak their minds, and yes, beautiful. Women should aspire to be these things so that men's desire to pursue is kindled" (pp. 187–188). The catch is that this is Mrs. Maken's understanding of what men look for in a wife. As admirable as the qualities above are, they are really not the primary attributes for an ideal wife. Many men want women who are feminine, submissive, complementary (spelled with an "e"), and complimentary (spelled with an "i"). They want women who are honest, nurturing, responsible, kind, merciful, patient, encouraging, conciliatory, and agreeable. They want women who are affectionate, playful, and fond of having sex with their husbands. I have said it before, and will say it again: Just because a man is serious about marriage doesn't mean he is serious about marrying a given woman. There are many "beautiful," "educated," women who are able to "speak their minds" and yet are total duds when it comes to the opposite sex. Shaming and blaming men will not get Debbie Maken's fans any closer to wearing bridal gowns if they don't have the qualities men find desirable, as opposed to just having the qualities Mrs. Maken finds desirable.

Wacky Precepts from the Past

Elsewhere, in chapter 14, Mrs. Maken quotes a couple of luminaries from the distant past in support of her tirades against single men. The quotes cited are really quite fanciful, if not downright nasty. For instance, Mrs. Maken notes, "Remember what John Calvin said? The man who chooses to stay single (without a specific call from God) is guilty of 'stealing' a husband from a wife" (p. 181). With all due respect to my readers in the Reformed camp, I don't think the *ipse dixits* of John Calvin are so sacrosanct that they cannot be scrutinized or even discarded. The notion of a single man "stealing a husband from a wife" is illogical and patently stupid. It is a gross case of begging the question. Which woman did the single man steal from? What right could the woman in question claim to the man in question? If she rejects him, is he still guilty of theft? If he choses to marry someone else, is he still guilty of theft? If there are more women than men, which women were stolen from and which women received ill-gotten gain? Theft implies taking something that was already the property of another person. If a man's life is already the property of a given woman, then why must he seek her out and impress her if he already belongs to her?

Yet as bad as John Calvin's alleged statement is about single men, it is cannot a hold a candle to the following stinker floated by Mrs. Maken:

> Erasmus said it well in his famous essay *In Praise of Marriage*: "[W]hat is more hateful than a man who, as though born for himself alone, lives for himself, looks out for himself, is sparing or lavish for himself, loves no one and is loved by no one? Indeed, should not such a monster be thought fit to be driven away from the general fellowship of mankind." In other words, he saw those who willfully choose singleness as useless drones and fruitless burdens on this earth who have no sense of obligation to follow the familial patterns of their parents or to sacrifice for another. (p. 182)

I ask in response "what is more hateful" than for a person to falsely accuse those who choose to be single of being unconcerned about others and to label these single people as being "useless drones" and "fruitless burdens." This kind of talk is reminiscent of the things Nazis used to say about Jews. Jesus Christ said that "out of the abundance of the heart the mouth speaks" (Matt. 12:34). I do not see anything pure or holy in the statement above above but only carnal disdain for those who dare to live differently. Really, Mrs. Maken doesn't earn any brownie points with me by dredging up the ignorant ideas of misguided religious figures who have long passed away from this earthly life. Some sentiments are best left buried with those who engendered them.

The Final Solution

Overall, if there is any statement in chapter 14 that reveals Debbie Maken's designs, it is this quote: "Women, our biggest challenge in holding men accountable and inspiring them to biblical manhood is that they often don't know any better. They don't understand that this issue goes beyond personal choice to being held accountable by God for failing to pursue his will for their lives. We have no choice but to educate men. I think it would certainly be better if it came from ministers, church leaders, parents, or other male friends, but many of them are not particularly aware of the problem either" (p. 182). I advise Mrs. Maken and any woman that agrees with her to give up the idea of educating us men. Otherwise, they will be defeated. We will drive them back like the Amalekites and Canaanites did the Israelites who rejected God at Kadesh. Why should I believe that God is with Mrs. Maken's female fans on this matter? At best, any posturing from them will merely signal to a self-respecting man that these women should be avoided since they are not marriage material. Mrs. Maken says, "There is no shortage of men; one woman's gain is not usually another woman's loss" (p. 183). I think there will indeed be a shortage of men if women insist on treating men in a disrespectful manner. And no, the male collaborators of these women will fare no better if they should choose to go up against their fellow brothers. After all, it's pretty hilarious for a guy to lecture others on manhood when he obviously allows his identity to be defined by women and doesn't do any thinking for himself. Such a man certainly doesn't bring to mind the qualities of self-confidence and intestinal fortitude that one thinks of when considering manhood.

Anyway, the rest of chapter 14 is essentially a rehash of matters I have already covered in previous installments of my critique: Mrs. Maken's misuse of biblical characters, her pointless complaints about the private nature of modern marriages, her alarmist notions about the negative economic and social impact of people choosing to be single, her misguided beliefs about the benefits of enlisting courtship agencies and limiting access men have to women, and her dim view towards male-female friendships. In closing, I should point out an unusual statement by Mrs. Maken at the end of chapter 14. She says, "We must be honest and admit that men don't hold all the blame for the way things are" (p. 188). I am somewhat surprised that Mrs. Maken would say this, and I must give credit to Mrs. Maken for her concession. However, given the overall tenor of her book, it's really too little, too late.

PART XVI

Conclusion

In the closing comments of *Getting Serious about Getting Married*, Debbie Maken notes: "If you have read this far, I assume your reaction will either be 'hate it' or 'love it.' No one walks away from my material lukewarm" (p. 189). Mrs. Maken is most certainly correct in that observation. Let me be candid and say that I hate her book. I may sound abrupt in stating that, but I am simply making an honest confession with no personal animosity towards Mrs. Maken herself. What diplomatic or conciliatory response can I give in my review of a work that takes a view of singleness, marriage, and manhood which is both misguided and disturbing? When a bull is turned loose in a china shop, someone is going to call the animal control professionals. I have therefore taken upon myself the burden of providing a much-needed corrective to Mrs. Maken's damaging message.

What's the Deal (Qui Bono)?

In the course of writing my review of Mrs. Maken's book, I came across an article in *Christianity Today* entitled "What Married Women Want." I found the following statements in the article to be noteworthy:

> My theory is that women are looking for, in general, husbands who provide them with emotional and financial support, and support to make the choices that they think are important for them and for their children. Women who have husbands who are good breadwinners have the freedom to decide what they want to do, whether that's to stay home with their kids, whether that's to work part time, or whether that's to pursue work that might be more meaningful but not particularly remunerative ...

> ... we're going to also continue to see what I call a neo-traditional model of family life. What I mean by neo-traditional is that it's progressive in a sense that men, particularly religious men, are investing more and more—especially in the emotional arena—in their wives and children. But it's traditional in that there's still some kind of effort to, in a sense, mark off who is the primary breadwinner and who is the primary nurturer. That may mean that both the husband and wife are working in the outside labor force, but there's still some effort to give the lead for breadwinning to the husband and the lead for nurturing to the wife.[1]

We see from this article that women want to expand their "options" whereas the only thing that seems to be expanded for men is the expectations placed upon them. This article claims that some women still want to be the "primary nurturer" in the household. What does such a statement mean? Is it referring to domestic chores? Our technologies have made these chores easier, and women still often complain that men don't do their share of the housework. Are these women referring to spending more time with their children? Don't most loving fathers want more time with their children, too? Moreover, can women in one breath bemoan men making more money than them, but in another breath express a preference for a husband who earns the main income for his family? What happens to the paycheck that men bring home anyway? I ask these questions, but as you might guess, they are not addressed by the article.

Debbie Maken's book seems to have something in common with the piece I quoted, namely, a particular viewpoint. I previously noted that in chapter 12 of *Getting Serious about Getting Married*, Mrs. Maken draws a comparison between male suitors and prospective employees in a job interview. Such a comparison reveals something, I believe, about Mrs. Maken's mindset and the mindset of many other women. Throughout the book, an emphasis is placed on the idea of men measuring up to the expectations of women. It's nothing new. Whether it be Debbie Maken, the article in *Christianity Today*, or some other discussion about relationships, our feminized culture at large has the same outlook: The worth of men is reckoned in terms of what they can or cannot do for the "fairer sex."

In contrast, there is a verse in the Bible that I wish to bring to the attention of my readers: "For man is not from woman, but woman from man. Nor was man created for the woman, but woman for the man" (1 Cor. 11:8–9). Your eyes may be tempted to skip past some of the elements of that passage, but notice what it says: "nor was man created for the woman." In light of this statement, it seems to me that Mrs. Maken and many others are looking through the wrong end of the telescope. Contrary to the popular notions that many have, men are not put on this earth to fulfill the dreams and aspirations of women. The question is not, as many would have it, what use women have for men. It is very much the opposite.

The sobering truth is that women were created to help men. This is not to say that women are useless apart from men, for I clearly affirm the inherent worth of all women, married or single. It is also not to say that men have a right to ignore the needs and concerns of the women in their lives. It is to say, however, that if a single man does not desire female companionship, then he should not have to apologize for his refusal to marry.

Marriage is Not Necessarily Desirable

I can hear my critics citing verses like "marriage should be honored by all" (Heb. 13:4) and "whoever finds a wife finds a good thing" (Prov. 18:22). They miss the point when they do so. I am not against marriage. Marriage is indeed ordained by God. Having said that, I remind my readers that even though the Bible says some positive things about marriage in principle, it does not guarantee a happy marriage for everyone (Prov. 12:4b; Prov. 25:24). Otherwise, we would not hear of the numerous heartbreaks experienced by godly people who have chosen to marry. If something is neither commanded nor forbidden by God, then the rule of expediency applies. Sometimes marriage is not expedient (1 Cor. 6:12; 1 Cor. 7:28). In other words, it does no good to discourse at length about the nutritional benefits of apples when the orchards have been sprayed with DDT.

If marriage is a slam-dunk conclusion, then why the strident, overbearing, paternalism that is too often found in the camp of the Marriage Mandate Movement? It smacks of desperation. There is an increasing number of men who are not taking the bait, and the status quo can no longer afford to ignore this fact. For many men, there is nothing compelling about an arrangement that seems to primarily benefit everybody and anybody except the fellow who was goaded into it.

Those pundits who extol marriage over singleness should remember the words of Ralph Waldo Emerson: "What you do speaks so loud I cannot hear what you say." Though people talk of "settling down," I see stressed-out and harried couples. Though people talk of marriage "broadening one's horizons," I see people scaling back their hopes and dreams as the obligations of marriage crowd into their lives. Though people talk about "marital bliss," I see couples who appear indifferent to each others company. Though people talk about marriage bringing "growth," "selflessness," and "maturity," I see families embroiled in the most petty, puerile, and malicious squabbles. Though people talk about a man "needing a helper," I see men who are belittled and taken advantage of by their wives. Though people talk about "honoring marriage," and getting serious about "commitment," I see divorces left and right. We cannot pretend that these developments are anomalies. Otherwise, I wouldn't be writing this book and we wouldn't scratching our heads about why younger generations are hesitant to get married.

Is the Young Man Safe?

What does marriage have to offer to men these days? Men are finding many of the expectations placed upon them to be suspect. Trying to pawn off such expectations as "biblical manhood" is ludicrous when men can see that the Scriptures have been misused in that respect. If all things were equal, the normal desire that men have for women would be a sufficient reason for matrimony, but all things are not equal. Men live in a world much different from the one in which Adam lived or even the one in which their grandparents lived. The mainstream media can no longer marginalize the voices of men on gender issues. Men have access to other venues of information, and therefore they are beginning to realize that they have more choices in life. Like it or not, family is just one choice among many for men. Men don't have to marry. They don't even have to date. Their happiness and worth does not depend upon women. Consequently, an increasing number of principled men are saying "No" to tying the knot, and some are even engaged in what can be called a "marriage strike."[2] The steep social costs of pursuing marriage make many men rightfully hesitant. For these men, the promise of intimacy and belonging in a close-knit community is often overshadowed by the ugly specter of possible exploitation.

Even if a man finds a godly woman to marry, he is still vulnerable in a way that single men are not. He is one paycheck away from having his family live in poverty. He lives day to day at the mercy of the the public school teacher, the social worker, the police, the family judge, and the politician, who may or may not have any respect for his position as a husband and/or father. If he decides to form a family, he becomes obliged to outsiders to ensure the survival of his household. He depends on society to act in good faith. The problem is that society often does not do so.

Whenever ordinary people get involved in get-rich-quick schemes or make rash decisions with their money, we rightfully question how responsible they have been in the stewardship of what God has given to them. We apply the sound principle of prudence and erring on the side of caution in so many aspects of life, yet we fling these principles right out the window when we admonish young men to marry. Men are asked to throw caution to the wind (though no one will admit this) and expend an increasing amount of their time, livelihood, and emotional well-being to chase the rabbits of romance for the uncertain promise of love. This is nonsensical. Too many people fail to appreciate that there is a limit to what we can expect of men in terms of sacrifice and risk-taking in order to obtain intimacy and commitment from women. In a society that has become hostile to men, that limit has most certainly been exceeded.

Where I live, many people are familiar with the destructive power of tornadoes. Recently, somebody told me a story of some people that were asked to take shelter inside a building when a tornado warning was issued. Some individuals, however, did not want to stay in the building because they had made previous plans to leave town. The foolishness of these individuals caused me to reflect on the attitude of so many towards marriage these days. Like the careless individuals who thought they could take their chances in bad weather, some would have men take their chances in a climate of misandry.

Conclusion

When Sugar and Spice Isn't That Nice

Men have not been in a habit of asking themselves what they want from a relationship. They have not always been encouraged to articulate their feelings about this matter; instead, they have been mostly trained to put the needs of others before themselves. Whether out of some notion of "chivalry" or a need to address the "past wrongs" of a "patriarchal culture," men have found themselves deferring to women in defining what a male-female relationship should look like. But the noble inclinations of men to be selfless and respectful of women are not always appropriate. Justice, decency, and propriety demand a limit to what women can rightfully ask of men. In fact, Christian men do a disservice to godly women when they declare all women to be worthy of the same treatment. *The honor we give to good women has no meaning unless we can boldly expose the deeds of those women who are dishonorable.* We need more men like Elijah to stand up against the Jezebels of our day and against the spineless Ahabs that do the bidding of these women (even the Ahabs in our churches).

Often, people say that men and women alike are at fault for the way they have treated each other. However, for the last three decades or so, we have tended to lay down the law for only one gender. Now, I think it is time for women to undertake the unconformable task of facing up to their own shortcomings and peccadilloes.

Women said men were the oppressors and that men operated from a default position of privilege. In response, men gave women opportunities that for generations many men never had. Men supported initiatives that granted preferential treatment to women, all to "remedy past inequities." Men modified their behaviors. What did women do? They slandered men as lechers, aggressors, stupid brutes, or obsolete beasts of burden. Men were shouted down when they tried to raise concerns about the charges made against them. They were often told to "be a man" in order to hush any protestations that could be made against the callousness of others. Women, on the other hand, gained an increasing amount of influence in society while still holding on to the perks and privileges of traditional sex roles. They were given options that men were not. In personal relationships, women assumed a considerable degree of power. Men silently retreated. Now some have the temerity to demand that men come back to the table even though the others seated there have acted in bad faith.

Can a woman have a realistic attitude about men and relationships when academia, government, popular culture, and religious pundits routinely validate her choices and offer little or no criticism of her behavior toward men? By way of analogy, can a child have a healthy attitude about life when its parents dote on it excessively? To ask these questions is to answer them. Those who constantly defer to contemporary women stand on shaky ground.

There is a consequence for the way women treat men. I suppose most men won't tell today's women that they are undesirable. Perhaps men just won't desire women enough to commit their lives to them. Debbie Maken may excoriate men for their withdrawal from society, but as I believe one man said, men get so used to disapproval over time that even approval doesn't matter.

The Loving Thing to Do?

I suspect some will counter that a man should lay aside whatever misgivings he might have about today's women, marriage, or about society's anti-male inclinations. They might say that men should "should just let go of their bitterness and fear" and "act out of love." Indeed, what would be the loving thing to do? Let us turn the question back on those who put it to men. Why don't the pundits become more loving and try to understand the problems men face instead of engaging in the kind of rhetoric that I find in Debbie Maken's book?

As it is, the word "love" may be used indiscriminately by our culture, but the biblical notion of love does not necessary imply the willingness to marry. Otherwise, shall we accuse women of being "unloving" when they reject the advances of men? What kind of benevolence can men expect from women in this manner? I have read somewhere of a prostitute who feel she serves a good cause by helping lonely, undesirable men who cannot find affection elsewhere. I suspect my audience would reject her mindset, so why assume that men are obligated to offer something similar to women? Biblical love focuses on the physical needs and spiritual needs of people. It is not about saving women from the single life or saving institutions from certain demographic realities.

What about the notion of "tough love"? When a father punishes his child, does it mean that he has stopped being loving? When God repeatedly punished the Israelites for their rebellion, did he act in a way that was contrary to his loving nature? The last time I checked, Ephesians 5:11 still said: "And have no fellowship with the unfruitful works of darkness, but rather expose them." Love doesn't mean enabling people in their wicked and destructive proclivities. In Debbie Maken's book, she notes that self-interest is not necessary selfishness. If that is the case, then religious men have a right to put biblical self-interest over enabling the selfishness of others. The loving thing that men can do is expose the misandry that has sadly crept into our churches. The loving thing that men can do is not compromise on their principles, even if it brings hardship on those who have failed to repent.

Who must repent? Besides many women, our churches and society as whole must repent. These agents have the broken the covenants they had with men. For each broken covenant, there is a respective curse. Our churches broke their covenant by failing to be places that encourage and edify men. They failed to be a spiritual family for not only married men, but single men as well. They became respecters of persons with regard to marital status and other matters. They haven't been too concerned about the loneliness and isolation of single men. The singleness of men seems to have now only become a "concern" in how it affects women and the bottom line of church treasuries. Churches have belittled men for the temptations that affect them in particular, but have offered no real solutions to the problems men face in seeking out positive alternatives. Churches most certainly have had little or nothing to say about how women mistreat men. The curse upon these churches is that men have left them in droves. These churches will suffer for lack of male leadership—and may even die.

Our society has broken its covenant with men by failing to protect the institution of marriage, by passing laws that undermine the position of men as husbands and fathers, by reducing men to an expendable commodity for the economic gain of others, and by marginalizing men at every turn in the public and private spheres of life. The curse upon society is that many men no longer obligate themselves to do anything beyond the bare minimum of what is required of them as citizens. They do not form families. They do not pursue excellence in workplaces that don't care about their input or welfare. They do not volunteer in communities that view them as a liability. Society will suffer as a result. Why should men care about a system that doesn't care about them? People who ignore this matter and yet pontificate all day long about men "refusing to take responsibility" are merely rearranging the chairs on the deck of the Titanic.

Some Closing Thoughts For My Critics

It would not surprise me in the least if, after reading what I have written, some accuse me of being unmerciful, unloving, unchristian, bitter, angry, anti-social, misogynistic, or having some emotional hang-ups. These baseless charges have been hurled at many good men that have gone before me. Even if these charges were true, my arguments demand an answer. I could have the most ungodly of motives in writing what I write and still what I say would have to be objectively weighed on the scales of truth. Simply put, cheap personal attacks accomplish nothing.

Debbie Maken and others indicate that the system is broken. True, but if we are going to fix it, then what I am saying needs to be considered. There are essentially two types of eligible men not getting married: those who don't want to marry and those who face obstacles in getting married. For the first group, we must prove that marriage can benefit them if we want to see them wedded. I have already made the case that they don't have a duty to marry, so the proverbial carrot will have to be used instead of the stick. Can we truly say there are benefits for men to marry these days? When some try to point out the benefits for men, they usually window-dress the responsibilities and the hardships of marriage as "opportunities for character building" or some other disingenuous psychobabble. Others, in an attempt to list some palpable benefits, confuse correlation with causality (e.g., they say married men are richer, healthier, and happier than single men without researching why this is the case). We have to do better than this, or at least people need to rethink their approach to marriage so that it truly does having some meaningful to offer to men.

For both groups of unmarried men, we must address the pitfalls and obstacles of getting married in the current cultural climate. If the perils of marriage dwarf the benefits of marriage, then we cannot expect men to embrace the institution. The issues that I touched upon in this review, and of which Debbie Maken and others seem to be so dismissive, are not going away anytime soon. We need to tackle the thorny issues of dwindling economic opportunities for men, the bitter fruit of feminism, women with unrealistic expectations, etc. Thinking men can redeem culture one marriage at a time is like thinking that if we plant enough roses in the desert sand, the soil will eventually become favorable to the flowers.

Women, in particular, have some things they need to do. They need to be more attuned to the challenges men face—and be more supportive of men. They need to stop taking their cues from feminists and even from supposedly "conservative" women who have an entitlement mindset. Women who want to get married should offer men praise (not blame), understanding (not accusations), and genuine interest (not cynical timetables). Women need to put Debbie Maken's book down on the table and instead listen to those good women who have a constructive understanding of how the sexes should relate to each other. Good women need to stand up for the honor of men who stand up for fairness in the face of hateful women and spineless men. We do not need to mention that men have mistreated women. Of course men have their responsibilities; that proverbial horse has been beaten to death. Rather, we need to encourage women to look in the mirror—to turn away from the dark path of gynocentrism and misandry that our worldly culture sets before them. We need to encourage women to turn to a better model of womanhood —not one pushed by sycophantic religious pundits, but one approved by God.

Let me also state that before pundits talk about "getting serious about getting married" they need to get serious about restoring marriage. How can they aim their cross-hairs at single men when there are so many loveless and joyless marriages in our society? Sermons are better lived than told. It's time for the apologists for marriage to stop talking the talk and start walking the walk. Baby Boomers and Gen Xers, in particular, have nothing of which to boast; the younger generations can look at their marriages and see one disas-

Conclusion

ter after another. It's time for those who would lead the way to "put up or shut up."

To a great extent, what I have written is descriptive, not prescriptive. I do not really demand a course of action as much as I lay forth some options on the table with their respective rewards and consequences. Cultural reactionaries can ignore what I have said, circle the wagons, and catechize the "true believers" in their midst, but they will gain no ground with those sitting on the proverbial fence. Will people prayerfully consider what I have written and test my convictions in the light of God's revealed word? Or will people summarily reject my thoughts without a fair hearing? As the Bible says, "He who has ears, let him hear."

NOTES

PART I
(Debbie Maken's Introduction to Her Book)

1. Candy Williams, "Psychologist Offers Help in Finding Your Soul Mate," *Pittsburgh Tribune-Review*, February 12, 2002, http://www.pittsburghlive.com/x/pittsburghtrib/s_16854.html (accessed May 7, 2007).
2. Vicki Fong, "Unhappy Marriages Detrimental to Self-Esteem and Health," *Medical News Today*, January 27, 2006, http://www.medicalnewstoday.com/medicalnews.php?newsid=36653 (accessed May 7, 2007).
3. "Happiness: Doctors Have It Down to a Science," *NBC5.com*, February 14, 2005, http://www.nbc5.com/irresistible/4195564/detail.html (accessed May 7, 2007).

PART II
(Ch. 1 - "What the Bible Says About Marriage")

1. John Calvin, *Commentaries on the Twelve Minor Prophets*, vol. 5, *Zechariah and Malachi*, trans. John Owen (1849; repr., Grand Rapids, MI: Eerdmans, 1950), 554–559.
2. Markus Zehnder, "A Fresh Look at Malachi ii 13–16," *Vetus Testamentum* 53, no. 2 (2003): 249 (emphasis mine).

PART III
(Ch. 2 - "What the Bible Says About Being Single")

1. C. K. Barrett, *The First Epistle to the Corinthians* (Peabody, MA: Hendrickson, 1968), 174–175.

2. Richard E. Oster, Jr., *1 Corinthians*, College Press NIV Commentary (Joplin, MO: College Press, 1995), 177.
3. Simon J. Kistemaker, *Exposition of the First Epistle to the Corinthians* (Grand Rapids, MI: Baker, 1993), 244 (emphasis mine).
4. Gordon Fee, *The First Epistle to the Corinthians,* NICNT (Grand Rapids, MI: Eerdmans, 1987), 278–290.
5. Ibid., 284.
6. Ibid., 348–349 (emphasis mine).

PART IV
(Ch. 3 - "Historical Views on Singleness")

1. For further discussion of John Calvin's treatment of religious dissenters and Sebastian Castellio's opposition to him, see Stefan Zweig, *The Right to Heresy: Castellio Against Calvin* (New York: Viking Press, 1936).
2. For further discussion of Martin Luther's animosity toward the Jews, see Roland H. Bainton, *Here I Stand: A Life of Martin Luther* (New York: New American Library, 1950), 296–298.
3. Martin Luther to Jerome Weller, in *The Life and Letters of Martin Luther,* ed. Preserved Smith (Boston: Houghton-Mifflin, 1914), 324–325.
4. Enuma Okoro, "Mixed Blessings," *Boundless*, July 13, 2006, http://www.boundless.org/2005/articles/a0001307.cfm (accessed July 2, 2007).
5. Albert Mohler, "Can Christians Use Birth Control?," *www.AlbertMohler.com*, May 08, 2006, http://www.albertmohler.com/commentary_read.php?cdate=2006-05-08 (accessed July 2, 2007).
6. See generally *A Select Library of Nicene and Post-Nicene Fathers of the Christian Church*, 1st ser., ed. Philip Shaff (Grand Rapids, MI: Eerdmans, n. d.), 3:413, 12:105; 2nd ser., ed. Phillip Shaff and Henry Wace (n. d.), 4:557, 5:345–348, 6:344–345.

PART V

(Ch. 4 - "The Lack of Male Leadership: The True Cause of Protracted Singleness")

1. Paul Nathanson and Katherine K. Young, *Spreading Misandry: The Teaching of Contempt for Men in Popular Culture* (Montreal: McGill-Queen's University Press, 2001).

2. "Women, Not Men, Are Primary Electronics Consumers," *Gizmag*, March 6, 2007, http://www.gizmag.com/go/6935/ (accessed August 11, 2007).

3. Angela Fiori, "To Single Men on Today's Women: Caveat Emptor," *LewRockwell.com*, June 28, 2001, http://www.lewrockwell.com/orig/fiori2.html (accessed August 11, 2007).

4. M. F. Brining and D. W. Allen, "'These Boots Are Made for Walking': Why Most Divorce Filers Are Women," *American Law and Economics Review* 2, no. 1 (2000): 126–169.

5. Donald G. Dutton and Tonia L. Nicholls, "The Gender Paradigm in Domestic Violence Research and Theory: Part 1—The Conflict of Theory and Data," *Aggression and Violent Behavior* 10 (2005): 680–714.

6. Peg Tyre, "The Trouble with Boys," *Newsweek*, June 30, 2006, http://www.msnbc.msn.com/id/10965522/site/newsweek/ (accessed August 13, 2007); Home School Legal Defense Association, "Home Schooling Achievement," HSLDA, http://www.hslda.org/docs/study/comp2001/HomeSchoolAchievement.pdf (accessed August 13, 2007).

7. Monica M. Moore and Diana L. Butler, "Predictive aspects of nonverbal courtship behavior in women," *Semiotica* 76, no. 3/4 (1989): 205–215.

8. Willard Harley, *His Needs, Her Needs* (Grand Rapids, MI: Revell, 2001), 183.

9. Camerin Courtney, "30 and Single? It's Your Own Fault," *Christianity Today*, June 21, 2006, http://www.christianitytoday.com/ct/2006/juneweb-only/125-32.0.html (accessed August 14, 2007).

10. G. M. Martinez et al., "Fertility, Contraception, and Fatherhood: Data on Men and Women from Cycle 6 (2002) of the National Survey of Family Growth," *Vital and Health Statistics*, ser. 23, no. 26 (May 2006): 68–69, http://www.cdc.gov/nchs/data/series/sr_23/sr23_026.pdf (accessed August 15, 2007).

PART X
(Ch. 9 - "'Being Single = Knowing and Serving God Better'")

1. Alex Chediak, "Open Letter to Andreas Köstenberger, " *www.alexchediak.com*, August 26, 2006, http://www.alexchediak.com/blog/2006/08/open_letter_to_andreas_kostenb.php (accessed August 27, 2007).

PART XI
(Ch. 10 - "'Single = Celibate'")

1. Stephen Arterburn et al., *Every Man's Battle: Winning the War on Sexual Temptation One Victory at a Time* (Colorado Springs, CO: Waterbrook Press, 2000), 40–41.
2. Ibid., 116–117.
3. A. H. Maslow, "Deprivation, Threat, and Frustration," *Psychological Review* 48 (1941): 365–366.
4. Eleanor Daniel, *What the Bible Says About Sexual Identity* (Joplin, MO: College Press, 1981), 235.
5. John Piper, "His Commandments Are Not Burdensome," *www.desiringgod.org*, http://www.desiringgod.org/ResourceLibrary/Sermons/ByDate/1985/492_His_Commandments_are_Not_Burdensome/ (accessed September 2, 2007).
6. *American Heritage Dictionary of the English Language*, 4th ed., s.v. "celibacy."
7. Arterburn et al., 112.
8. Daniel, 234–235.

PART XII
(Ch. 11 - "A Few More 'Easy' Answers")

1. Michael Medved, "Journalistic Malpractice in 'Marriage is Dead' Report," *Townhall.com*, January 18, 2007, http://www.townhall.com/columnists/MichaelMedved/2007/01/18/journalistic_malpractice_in_marriage_is_dead_report (accessed September 2, 2007).

PART XIII
(Ch. 12 - "Saying No to the Dating Game")

1. Roberto Rivera y Carlo, "Optional Anxiety," *Boundless*, February 1, 2007, http://www.boundless.org/2005/articles/a0001440.cfm (accessed October 30, 2007).

PART XIV
(Ch. 13 - "Enlisting Agency")

1. Victor H. Matthews, *Manners and Customs in the Bible* (Peabody, MA: Hendrickson, 1991), 21.
2. Joel F. Drinkard, "An Understanding of Family in the Old Testament: Maybe Not as Different from Us as We Usually Think," *Review and Expositor* 98 (Fall 2001): 486–493.
3. David Noel Freedman, ed., *The Anchor Bible Dictionary* (New York: Doubleday, 1992), 4:560–562.
4. Matthews, 24.
5. Francis Brown et al., *A Hebrew and English Lexicon of the Old Testament* (London: Oxford, 1968), 592.
6. Michael Lawrence, "Real Men Risk Rejection," *Boundless*, February 8, 2007, http://www.boundless.org/2005/articles/a0001443.cfm (accessed August 2, 2008).
7. Mary Haweis, *The Art of Beauty* (New York: Harper and Brothers, 1878), 262–263.

8. Patricia H. Shiono and Linda Sandham Quinn, "Epidemiology of Divorce," *The Future of Children* 4, no. 1 (1994): 16.
9. Blaine Harden, "Numbers Drop for the Married With Children," *Washington Post*, March 4, 2007, http://www.washingtonpost.com/wp-dyn/content/article/2007/03/03/AR2007030300841.html (accessed August 3, 2008).
10. Daniel Amneus, *The Garbage Generation* (Alhambra, CA: Primrose Press, 1990), 121.

PART XVI
(Conclusion)

1. Brad Wilcox, "What Married Women Want," interview by Stan Guthrie, *Christianity Today*, November 13, 2006, http://www.christianitytoday.com/ct/2006/october/53.122.html (accessed August 23, 2008).
2. Wendy McElroy, "The Marriage Strike," *Fox News*, August 12, 2003, http://www.foxnews.com/story/0,2933,94415,00.html (accessed August 23, 2008).

Made in the USA
Lexington, KY
15 November 2014